Help! I Think My Loved One Is an Alcoholic

Help! I Think My Loved One Is an Alcoholic

A SURVIVAL GUIDE FOR LOVERS, FAMILY, AND FRIENDS

Michelle S. Fondin

ISBN-13: 9781539474326
ISBN-10: 1539474321

Author's note
All the stories in this book are based on actual experiences.

The Twelve Steps are reprinted with permission of Alcoholics Anonymous World Services Inc., (AAWS). Permission to reprint the Twelve Steps does not mean that AAWS has reviewed or approved the contents of this publication, or that AAWS necessarily agrees with the views expressed herein. AA is a program of recovery from alcoholism only-use of the Twelve Steps in connection with programs and activities, that are patterned after A.A. but that address other problems, does not imply otherwise.

Cover design by Jay M. Fondin

Dedication

This book is dedicated to the person I love. You know who you are. So proud of you for fighting this battle. Much love.

Acknowledgments

Thank you to all the people in recovery who helped make this book possible. In particular, thank you to Tim, Raul, Rachel, Tiffany, Waldon, Dan and Lee. Thank you so much for taking the time to share your stories with me and to help me see the beauty in recovery. Thank you to Jay Fondin for creating an amazing cover.

The Serenity Prayer

God, grant me the serenity to accept the things I cannot change,
The courage to change the things I can,
And the wisdom to know the difference.

Contents

Preface

ntrigued by the title or desperate for help from pain, you picked up this book for a reason. If you're wondering whether or not your loved one is an alcoholic, by the time you've come to the point of searching for a book on the subject, chances are he or she is, in fact, an alcoholic. You see, our denial of our loved one's alcoholism, is often just as strong as the alcoholic's denial. And by the time we've come to terms with exactly what's going on, it's usually been going on for quite some time. As you will learn, the disease of alcoholism, disguises itself in many ways. Addiction is nothing new. However, since alcohol is so prevalent in our society, it's easy to dismiss abnormal drinking behavior with societal norms.

There is little mainstream information on how exactly to understand alcoholism and the person behind the disease. Much information in the media vilifies the alcoholic, and criminalizes his behavior. To attribute total darkness to the alcoholic as if he's doomed for a life sentence is to not fully grasp the complexity of the illness and gives little hope for redemption. To not understand your role (yes, I did say *your role*) in the process is to keep yourself rooted in the victim mindset and in the end, will help no one.

It is my hope to bring enlightenment to you and to all who truly love an alcoholic. I wish to not only bring understanding of the inner workings of the disease but also to bring love, compassion, forgiveness, strength, and vision. In order to fight and win this battle, you must know what and who are you are dealing with. You can win the battle of alcoholism and so can your loved one. But the terrain of survival is going to look very differently than any other you've ever fought on. The rules that apply to normal life, don't apply in addiction. The strategies that work in normal relationships don't make sense to a drinking alcoholic. If you are unfamiliar with the territory, much of this will seem strange at the first go. If you do not suffer from addiction, it will seem downright counterintuitive. And if you are the compassionate sort (like me), you will have to become a compassionate (pardon my French) hard ass.

We are going on a journey here. It's a journey to fully comprehending and surviving a relationship with an alcoholic whether that person is your husband, wife, boyfriend, girlfriend, best friend, brother, sister, son, daughter, mother or father. We will analyze the disease they possess from the inside out and from the outside in. We will pinpoint behaviors, triggers, and signs and give you a head's up as to what to look for and how to overcome the devastating effects of this illness.

To this end, I'm going to ask you to visualize something in your mind right now. Throughout this book, keep this vision and when interacting with your actively drinking alcoholic, actually see the vision. If you are going to truly survive the relationship with your alcoholic loved one and actually save the relationship, you *must* see him or her as a loving person who is worthy of receiving love, compassion and forgiveness. Your alcoholic loved one *is* worthy of all those things. You might not feel it now. You might feel anger, frustration or even hatred toward him or her. Know that there is not any one right emotion to feel toward your alcoholic right now. What I'm hoping is that by the end of this book, you will be able to feel love, compassion and forgiveness for your alcoholic even if you are no longer in a relationship with him or her. You will have that understanding from a cellular level so that *you* can heal first.

Next, you must visualize the alcoholism, the disease, as a third party. When I'm helping people to fully grasp the "why" in the madness of alcoholism, I often refer to the disease as a small person, like a little green alien (Did you ever see the movie *Alien?*), taking over your loved one. When things are really difficult to understand, imagine the little green monster or alien, actually taking over your loved one's words, actions, desires, emotions, and drive. That little green alien is shrewd, conniving, and extremely convincing. Once you understand the chemistry of addiction, you will know why I've chosen to look at the disease as a third party in your relationship. In the beginning with my loved one, I referred to the alcoholism as a mistress. My loved one was appalled that I would call the addiction as such, even though that's what it felt like at the time. However, this can't apply to all relationships. So I like the green alien monster image. It also seems to help others understand because we've all seen cartoons, science fiction, or horror movies.

Finally, throughout the book, I will be referring to the alcoholic as him or her and he or she interchangeably. Whatever resonates for you, plug it in your mind. I will also use the term "your alcoholic" to refer to your alcoholic loved one. This is simply a term of endearment I've coined in writing about alcohol addiction and does not imply disrespect in any way. And last but not least, I realize that you are probably hurting; not only mentally, emotionally and spiritually but some of you are suffering physically as well. If you are in a dangerous situation, make sure to get out and take any children under eighteen-years-old with you. Some alcoholics never get violent, many do. But there is no book that will get you out of a violent situation; you must do that yourself. Then, once you're safe, you can read this to start your healing and hopefully your alcoholic loved one will also get the help that he or she needs to heal too.

I'm going on this journey with you, on this survival trek, because I've been there and still am sometimes. You see; addiction, even in recovery, is a life long journey for families, friends, lovers and the addict. Things can and do get better and alcoholics do recover but that little green alien monster will still be there, even though he may be locked in a cage.

Stay strong and move forward. If you've survived this long, in an alcoholic household or relationship, you're already a survivor. Now, you'll just be a happier and more peaceful one.

My Story and How I Got Here: Loving an Alcoholic

've been into grocery stores thousands of times and never noticed the display that is so prominent as you enter the store. Not once had I ever given it a glance, not ever, until I had an alcoholic in my life.

The first time I noticed the display of wine bottles, hundreds of them, staring at me as they penetrated the main aisle, I was astounded. There was no avoiding them and I had to purposefully push my shopping cart around them to get away. Then I experienced the sickening feeling in my stomach as anger arose within me. "How?" I said inside myself, "How can someone who has a drinking problem ever get away from this? It's everywhere and it's in your face all the time."

Most of my life, I had never really known someone with a drinking problem. Oh, of course I knew some people in my past but we weren't close. There was my uncle who was always drunk on holidays or my first boyfriend's alcoholic mother. But those people didn't affect my life. And in my head, they were just mean, unruly people who were careless and irresponsible.

Then I met Johnny*[1]. Johnny was unlike anyone I had ever met before. He was funny, lighthearted, and fun to be around. He was also deep, affectionate, and caring. Johnny was so interesting to talk to and a real friend when I needed him. My connection to Johnny was incredible. Soon after we met, we were inseparable. It seemed that everyone knew and liked Johnny. Everywhere we went people knew him. And it was great being with such a fun guy.

After several weeks, I noticed some strange behavior that I couldn't pinpoint. Johnny would make us a drink and when I accidentally took his instead of mine, I tasted an entire glass filled with alcohol and not just a mixed drink. Then one night, when Johnny brought over a bottle of wine in the middle of the week, he drank the whole thing when I said I didn't want any.

Since I wasn't aware of alcoholic behavior, it took me several more weeks before I realized that Johnny had a problem. And when I confronted him, he promised me he'd stop drinking for a month. In the midst of that month, he was sneaking drinks the whole time. But I didn't know it. I didn't realize it, until something big happened and I found several empty bottles of alcohol with a recently dated receipt.

My emotions ran from from denial to anger, to blame, to judgment, to disappointment, and back to anger again. None of it mattered. What I realized was that Johnny couldn't stop drinking. He was addicted.

What baffled me the most was that I had managed to get through decades of life without actually knowing what alcoholism truly is. I didn't know the warning signs. I didn't know how to handle the situations I found myself in. And I didn't understand how all of Johnny's

1 Names of friends & family are changed here to keep anonymity.

friends, who knew him well, had never confronted him on his problem. How could they not see it? I wondered.

I immersed myself in books about alcoholism to understand the disease. I went to Al Anon meetings to try and understand how to help myself and in turn be able to help him.

But still, the looming problem was being able to understand Johnny as a person who was suffering from the disease of alcohol addiction. The world out there judges alcoholics, as I did in my past with people I wasn't close to. According to most, they are irresponsible, arrogant, out of control, loud, and boisterous. And to family members they are often referred to as abusive, lying, cheating, and manipulating. While all of these descriptions of alcoholic behavior may and are true at times, these words do not describe the person.

Johnny is a person with great qualities. Sober, Johnny is intelligent, loving, and kind. Johnny is conscientious and wouldn't hurt anyone. But the part that is difficult to understand is that when Johnny drinks, he becomes someone he is not.

As a person who loves an alcoholic, it's hard to separate and make the difference between the person we love and the person who suffers from a disease. Believe me, I've run the gamut of feelings about my alcoholic and his situation. I've read many books that tell you how to "handle" the problem drinker or to ignore her behavior. You will definitely get tips in this book on how to handle certain situations and behaviors but I want to take it deeper. Other books take a hands off approach and explain that you simply have to let your alcohol addicted loved one hit rock bottom. I couldn't take a "hands off" approach, even though I tried. I truly love Johnny and didn't want to abandon him. I needed to figure out how to love him without enabling his addiction. I wanted to know what goes on inside of him. But I could find little information on what goes on in the alcoholic's heart, mind and soul.

It's my belief that if we don't seek to understand the heart, mind and soul of the person who suffers, we will never truly understand the disease.

I took the stance that it's time to bring to light the disease of alcoholism from the perspective of the patient because that is, *who* he is. He is not a bum, a lazy person, or an irresponsible member of society. He is one who suffers at the deepest cellular level. She is the person who needs to be saved from herself if she is to live. And she needs and deserves the compassion and understanding of family members and friends.

With Johnny, I found I was embarrassed to tell family and friends about his problem. I felt that way because on a societal level, we still feel it's embarrassing. No one really talks about the alcoholics in their families. Now, I feel that the diagnosis of alcoholism should be no more embarrassing or shameful than a diagnosis of cancer, heart disease, stroke, or Alzheimer's.

In addition, there needs to be greater training in the medical field on how to detect alcoholism in a patient by a simple, but precise questionnaire. When Johnny shared with his general practitioner that his family was concerned about his drinking, his physician told him it was O.K. to have a couple of drinks per night. (Not knowing that Johnny's "couple" of drinks equaled at least ten shots of vodka or more.) Another physician prescribed pain-killing medications with nine refills to Johnny without even questioning if he had a problem with alcohol. And all Johnny had to do was complain about some joint pain to get the prescription. None of that should have ever occurred.

On a social level, we need to have sensitivity training in the work place on alcoholism, so employees don't feel pressured to drink in order to fit in or close the deal. And in our families we need to keep conversations open about alcohol use and abuse and to be able to talk about it without shame.

Alcohol rehab needs to become as commonplace and available as chemotherapy for cancer. There should be no more fear about public or private scorn when the word alcoholism is used.

I got here because I strive to understand both sides, the side of the person who suffers from the disease of alcoholism and how you, who loves an alcoholic, can get your life back. To get this perspective (since I'm not an alcoholic), I've interviewed several men and women at all stages of recovery, from 2 years to 8 years of recovery. You will read various aspects of their stories, which will help you, in turn, gain greater understanding of your alcoholic.

Since alcoholism is a family disease, your experience, in being directly involved in the life of an alcoholic, mirrors the disease itself. Every symptom, defeat, and every bit of chaos is in your life too, until you enter into recovery. It's not as simple as walking away. The deep-seated impressions have marked your life in a way that can only be dealt with through a program similar to that of an alcoholic in recovery.

Each chapter will be a work in progress for you as you understand the disease and how to heal. This work certainly doesn't replace the need for 12-Step meetings or therapy, but it's a good place to start. I've come a long way since Johnny and I met. After several years I feel bolder, stronger and much closer to my Higher Power. Most of all, I feel a deep sense of serenity and peace that I never had prior to knowing Johnny. It's my hope that you too achieve the peace and serenity in your life when it comes to your relationship with your alcoholic loved one.

Introduction

If there's just one message today, I believe it's about opening hearts. We must change the way America thinks about addiction and about those tens of millions whose lives are turned upside down by this health and human rights crisis. They are our sons and our daughters, our wives and husbands, our friends and neighbors, they are just us. And they deserve our love and our help.

— JIM HOOD, CO-FOUNDER AND DIRECTOR OF UNITE TO FACE ADDICTION ON OCTOBER 4, 2015

According to the National Council on Alcoholism and Drug Dependence, our nation's number one health problem is alcoholism and drug dependence.[2] Alcohol is the most commonly used addictive substance in the United States and 32.6 million adults suffer from alcohol use disorder in a 12-months span or

---

2 Ericson Nels, "Substance Abuse: The Nation's Number One Health Problem," OJJDP Fact Sheet, May 2001, 17, https://www.ncjrs.gov/pdffiles1/ojjdp/fs200117.pdf.

68.5 million adults over the course of their lifetime.[3] And this statistic is reserved for alcoholism. A common secondary addiction, that occurs in many who suffer from alcoholism, is prescription drug abuse. The National Institute on Drug Abuse estimated, in 2010, that 7 million Americans abused prescription drug medication.[4] If we were to include recreational drugs the accumulative statistic would be even higher.

An alcoholic has, on average, five people in his life who enable him or suffer the consequences of his drinking. Upon calculating this mathematical equation, about one in three Americans is directly affected by alcohol abuse or addiction.

With a disease that is so prevalent and present in our every day lives, how is it that so little is known or talked about?

A Socially Acceptable Drug

For the most part, alcohol is socially accepted as normal and interwoven into our daily lives. Business deals are sealed over a couple of drinks. Weddings, anniversaries and milestone birthdays are celebrated with a toast. And sporting events can seem flat and boring without that six pack. Drinking alcohol is often seen as a rite of passage. And those who choose not to socially drink are often socially scorned or pressured into having "just one". In fact, alcohol is accepted as a part of every day life. Each year the liquor industry spends almost $2 billion dollars on

---

3 Bridget F. Grant, PhD, "Alcohol Use Disorder Is Widespread, Often Untreated in the United States," JAMA Psychiatry, June 3, 2015, http://archpsyc.jamanetwork.com/article.aspx?doi=10.1001/jamapsychiatry.2015.0584
4 "Topics in Brief: Prescription Drug Abuse." National Institute on Drug Abuse http://www.drugabuse.gov/publications/topics-in-brief/prescription-drug-abuse

advertising and encouraging the consumption of alcoholic beverages.[5] And Americans spend over $90 billion dollars total on alcohol each year. Needless to say, alcohol is big business.

A Shroud of Shame

While the effects of alcoholism involve over a third of us, alcohol abuse and dependence still wears a shroud of shame. Those of us affected make excuses such as, "Oh he just had a rough day and is releasing stress." Or "The kids were just driving me crazy and I had to have a couple glasses of wine to calm my nerves." Because alcohol is so prevalent in our daily lives, we tend to overlook the warning signs of alcohol abuse and dependence. Friends and family tend to think that an alcoholic is someone "out there" who is homeless, unemployed, impoverished, and dirty. But my best friend, my wife, or my sister couldn't possibly be an alcoholic because she still has her job and she pays her bills on time. Howard B. Moss, M.D. stated, "We find that young adults comprise the largest group of alcoholics in this country, and nearly 20% of alcoholics are highly functional and well-educated with good incomes."[6]

And when we cannot ignore the fact that our loved one indeed has a drinking problem, there is an enormous air of shame that surrounds this fact. Because so many myths surround alcoholism, we as a society, still haven't socially accepted that alcoholism is, in fact, a

---

5 "Advertising spending of the beer, wine and liquor industry in the United States in 2013, by Medium'" (in thousand U.S. dollars), http://www.statista.com/statistics/245318/advertising-spending-of-the-alcohol-industry-in-the-us-by-medium/.

6 "Breaking Myths About Alcoholism," December 13, 2011, Betty Ford Center, http://www.bettyfordcenter.org/recovery/addiction/breaking-myths-about-alcoholism.php

disease and not a moral and personal failing. Those who love an alcoholic know all too well the burden of covering up an alcoholic's actions to spare the embarrassment of their behavior.

Ignorance is Bliss. Well, Sort Of.

Because of the stigma surrounding this common yet seemingly obscure disease, is the steadfast belief that somehow the alcoholism is due to a lack of willpower. We tend to think, if only he could drink solely on weekend nights, or if only she could control it around the kids. Well, he seems to know enough not to drink and drive. Or even, he's only gotten one DUI and it was bad luck. The cop was undercover and he was just going ten miles over the speed limit. With alcoholism, the less we know, as loved ones, the less we need to put our loving alcoholic into the category that we so fear.

And the alcoholic himself is amazingly convincing. His explanations are seamless and his arguments strong. So why shouldn't you believe him? He's got it under control.

Yet, simmering under the surface everyone knows the reality and it's too embarrassing to even admit it.

A Moral Failing?

It is true that drunkenness causes behavioral changes that often lead to police involvement and arrests. Abuse, physical and emotional, occurs under the influence. Alcohol addicts are known to take the wheel and cause fatal accidents. These are real and unfortunate consequences of alcoholism.

However, we must remember that the alcoholic is a person who is suffering severely from a disease. Time spent in jail or prison will not heal him. It may only make him worse. Mental diseases aside, an alcoholic, when sober, would likely not perform the illegal behavior he carries out when under the influence.

In my experience, these individuals, who suffer from alcoholism, are extra polite and conscientious when sober. In their moments of sobriety, extreme guilt takes over and they purposefully show their "good side" as a way to try and make amends.

As a society, we need to shift away from the mentality that the alcoholic is a bad person. Certainly there are immoral people whether alcoholic or not, but as a general rule, the actions caused by the drinking alcoholic are a direct consequence of the drinking and thus, the disease itself. So we must remember, the alcohol-addicted person is a sick person and not a bad one.

A Sick Person Gets Help Right?

The simple answer is "yes". But for the alcoholic, the answer is "yes, but..."

If you have flu symptoms you may run to your doctor for some relief. Or if you have an acute appendix attack, you will go to the hospital to get it removed. As you will read in the following stories, the alcoholic doesn't believe she is ill at all. And that is the baffling part about the entire illness. As an addiction interventionist once said to me, "It's a disease that tells you it's not a disease."

CHAPTER 1

What Is Alcoholism?

Researchers and medical professionals, in medical journals as early as 1784, wrote about alcoholism as an addiction. It was described as the irresistible desire to consume alcohol coupled with withdrawal symptoms and its destructive effects.[7] But it wasn't until 1933, shortly after the end of prohibition in the United States, that alcoholism was listed as a disease in the Standard Classified Nomenclature of Diseases and approved by the American Medical Association and the American Psychiatric Association.[8] The classification of alcoholism as a disease raised legal questions, namely, whether or not treatment costs should and must be covered under health insurances. Two years later, an organization that would help millions of people addicted to alcohol become sober, was formed. That organization, Alcoholics Anonymous, still helps millions more today, around the globe, to get and stay sober.

---

7 Karl Mann and Herminn Drik, "One Hundred Years of Alcoholism: The Twentieth Century," (Oxford University Press: January 1, 2000), http://alcalc.oxfordjournals.org/content/35/1/10.

8 M. Keller, "The disease concept of alcoholism revisited," Journal of Studies on Alcohol,1976, 37, 1694–1717.

Alcoholism is described as a neurobiological and psychosocial disease. In any case, it's a disease that affects a person on all levels: physically, psychologically, emotionally, socially, and spiritually.

A person addicted to alcohol will have problems controlling his or her drinking, becomes preoccupied with alcohol, has an increased tolerance for alcohol over time, and will continue to drink regardless of the consequences. An alcohol-addicted person will also experience withdrawal symptoms if he or she stops drinking.[9] Examples of withdrawal symptoms when an alcoholic significantly lowers the amount of alcohol he consumes or stops suddenly include: anxiety, irritability, agitation, nausea, vomiting, headaches, insomnia, tremors, seizures, or delirium tremens (DTs). Therefore, a person who has been addicted to alcohol, for weeks, months or years should never stop drinking without proper medical supervision because alcohol withdrawal syndrome can potentially be life threatening.

In medical books, alcoholism is defined as a chronic, progressive, and fatal disease. Firstly, it is a chronic disease like diabetes or heart disease, which means that it stays with the person, even after treatment. Treatment is needed to arrest the disease and to keep it from becoming worse. Secondly, alcoholism is a progressive disease, which means that over time, it will get more serious. And finally, it is a fatal disease. Left untreated, alcoholism ultimately leads to death.

The Nature Versus Nurture Debate

Even after scientific evidence to the contrary, some people still believe that excessive alcohol use and abuse is a question of will power, therefore a moral failing and a choice that the alcoholic refuses to make

---

9 The Mayo Clinic Staff, "Alcohol Use Disorder: Symptoms," http://www.mayoclinic.org/diseases-conditions/alcohol-use-disorder/basics/symptoms/con-20020866 .

toward sober living. Let me assure you that nothing could be further from the truth. And if you are a family member or a friend of an alcoholic, it is a slippery slope to believe he is consciously choosing addiction. A person who is addicted to alcohol has become physically and chemically dependent on the drug. They may have had a choice to take the first drink or the second, but once their bodies are chemically dependent, it no longer becomes a choice. They are a prisoner to alcohol until the alcohol has been completely cleared of their bodies and most often, once they receive medical help. The alcohol not only makes the alcoholic physically dependent, but he is also mentally and psychologically dependent.

In the 1990s, the National Institute of Alcohol Abuse and Alcoholism (NIAAA) and the Collaborative Study on the Genetics of Alcoholism (COGA), launched a study to identify the genes that may cause alcoholism.[10] They discovered a link to alcohol dependence on chromosomes 1 and 7 and a modest link on chromosome 2. Researchers have also pinpointed genes that may inhibit someone from becoming alcohol dependent. In people, who do not become alcohol dependent, there is a gene that releases an enzyme that rapidly breaks down alcohol in the body and releases a toxic chemical called, acetaldehyde. This chemical makes the drinker sick and flushed. The effects are so unpleasant that the person will stop after a small amount of alcohol. Acetaldehyde also comes into play when studying brain chemistry in an alcoholic. Researchers have discovered that acetaldehyde, in an alcoholic's brain, combines with other chemicals to produce compounds called TIQs. TIQs give a morphine-like effect,

---

10 Barry Youngerman and Heath Dingwell PhD., *The Truth About Alcohol*, DWJ Books LLC, 2010, pages 66-67.

which may explain the highly addictive quality of alcohol on the alcoholic brain.

Another study in 2009, involving identical twins and also adopted children, shows, that there is no doubt that a genetic component to alcoholism is real and present. There are, however, environmental factors that come into play and the disease of alcoholism includes both.

Why Does the Alcoholic Drink?

In a nutshell, he drinks because he has to.

No one really knows what causes the alcoholic to take the first drink. The stories on the following pages will reveal recovering alcoholics' stories of their first drink, but even those do not pinpoint a single cause. Many believe a traumatic experience in childhood or early adulthood causes a person, with a genetic predisposition toward alcoholism, to drink and then crave the euphoric sensation it gives her. But in reality, many give the account of no real trauma before drinking. And yet, others tell stories of hating the taste of alcohol the first, second and even third time. Since we've deducted that alcoholism, does in fact, run in families, a great number of alcoholics grew up in homes where one or both parents were also alcohol dependent. Trauma can take place in many forms and doesn't necessarily drive a person to drink alcohol.

A greater and more realistic explanation of why an alcoholic drinks is in understanding what happens in the brain of an alcoholic.

Alcohol causes a series of chemical reactions in the brain that interrupts its normal patterns. In other words, alcohol literally hijacks the brain causing the person to crave alcohol over anything else including food or water. Imagine a moment when you were really thirsty and didn't have any water nearby. Or imagine a time you were extremely hungry and you simply couldn't function until you put food in your stomach. Do you remember how it felt? Do you recall being completely obsessed with only getting food or water and being grouchy, irritable, and even unbearable until those needs were satisfied? That is what alcohol does to the brain of an alcoholic.

Among others, two normal neurotransmitters, in the brain, that are affected by alcohol addiction are dopamine and endorphins. Both of these neurotransmitters signal a sense of wellbeing in the body when we do something pleasurable. These neurotransmitters are linked to our survival since they are released when we eat, satisfy our need to drink water or have sex. These basic survival needs are hardwired in the limbic system (the thalamus and hypothalamus) and insure the survival of the human species. Alcohol hijacks the brain into believing that it's not food, water or sex that is the most necessary for survival, it's alcohol. Here's how it works, alcohol signals to the brain to produce less dopamine on its own. So when a person addicted to alcohol stops drinking, his levels of dopamine are way below what they need to be. Thus, naturally his sense of wellbeing is also low. The brain then sends out a signal that it will not survive unless more alcohol is taken in to elevate the levels of these crucial neurotransmitters back to their normal levels. Another neurotransmitter affected by alcohol consumption is serotonin, which is responsible for our sense of happiness. Alcohol also artificially elevates levels of serotonin initially, then the levels drop dramatically when the effects of alcohol wear off, leaving the alcoholic feeling depressed.

Once the limbic system in the alcoholic brain changes, his prefrontal cortex also changes. The prefrontal cortex is responsible for our self-control. So not only is his brain telling him he cannot survive without alcohol, his prefrontal cortex no longer allows him to have the impulse to say "no" to the substance.

To make matters more complicated, once the brain has been chemically modified, abnormal patterns of the brain's, otherwise normal activity, have been established. Suppose now, in a moment of enlightenment, the alcoholic decides it's time to stop the madness and get sober. She makes the conscious choice to not drink for the day. She has already overcome the incredible, inexplicable urge to drink and also harnessed some of the waning self-control that her now, weak prefrontal cortex is allowing her to experience. Again, to try to immerse yourself in this experience imagine you are overcoming the strong urge to drink water in a moment of dehydration. Your body needs water, it craves water, and your bodily functions start to suffer as a consequence of not getting water. Now the alcoholic has gone several hours and perhaps a day without drinking alcohol. Since the body is no longer used to going without alcohol, it retaliates. The brain goes haywire. She now experiences confusion, shakiness, nausea, headaches, tremors and anxiety. She may even experience seizures and hallucinations. The physical and psychological symptoms are so severe that she is likely to take a drink just to alleviate the symptoms. And so the vicious cycle continues.

Modifications in the brain of an alcoholic exceed explanations given here. But for the sake of understanding why the alcoholic drinks, I hope I've created a clearer picture.

Now extend this reasoning to why alcoholism is not a moral failing. Go back to the example of you being deprived of food and water. What wouldn't you do to obtain those vital items if you didn't have access to them? Would you lie, cheat or steal? Would you manipulate or coerce to simply get the food or water you so desperately needed? Once you got your basic needs met, you would go back to being a normal person with morals wouldn't you?

What I'm trying to help you understand is that non-addicted people under normal circumstances usually act in accordance with societal norms and under a certain moral code. If you act out of line, it's normal that you pay the consequences for your actions.

Now take a person, whose brain has been completely modified by alcohol (or any brain modifying drug substance) and ask them to behave exactly like a person, who is not under the influence, does. It is nearly impossible to expect that person to act, react, and make sane decisions when his brain is not capable of behaving the same.

Lack of Willpower is Never a Factor in Alcoholism

Even in light of all scientific evidence that points to the fact that alcoholism is indeed a brain disease, people still hold the belief that alcoholics lack willpower. And if they just had more of it, they could control the alcohol intake and function as normal human beings do. Nothing could be further from the truth.

I have interviewed many recovering alcoholics and as a whole, they are among the most persistent, goal-oriented, disciplined, driven, and tenacious set of people I've met. It simply comes down to the fact that all of these qualities, for many years, pointed to one single goal, getting more alcohol. Having lived with or having known an alcoholic for a period of time, you understand that he will go to great lengths to achieve his goal. His brain is able to divide, partition, and multitask to get to this goal. He is the best sales person, the most charming motivator and successful achiever in attainment. If you had his willpower toward another end goal, imagine what you would be achieving.

Your alcoholic has the willpower within him. However, the disease is so strong, he cannot use his gifts and talents to achieve a different goal unless he comes to a realization that he needs to change. And that breaking point typically comes when he hits rock bottom and comes to a spiritual awakening.

Is Abstinence the Only Answer?

I've already ascertained that the brain of an alcoholic reacts differently to alcohol than non-alcoholics. Also, I've outlined that constant use of alcohol changes brain chemistry. Finally, I've defined alcoholism as a chronic, progressive and fatal disease. Based on this information, you make the decision.

There have been movements by recovering alcoholics trying to prove that managed drinking is possible. In fact, there was a best-selling book by an author, a recovering alcoholic, who "proved" that she could manage drinking and not go back to binge and excessive drinking. She later confessed that she had been lying the entire time and that she, in fact, could not control it.

The confusion perhaps, lies in the difference between a heavy drinker and an alcoholic. Heavy drinkers, somehow, may never cross the line into alcoholism. Have heavy drinkers been able to modify their drinking habits? The answer is, "Yes, absolutely." But once a heavy drinker has crossed the line into alcoholism, it ceases to become a habit and enters the realm of no other choice but to drink.

Who Is the Alcoholic?

The alcoholic is your neighbor, your friend, your congressman, your child's teacher, or your doctor. Alcoholism knows no boundaries and does not discriminate. It has no particular degree or socio-economic status. Do not fool yourself into thinking that education, money, religion or friendships can prevent alcoholism. Alcoholism is an equal opportunity disease.

CHAPTER 2
You Love an Alcoholic. But Who Are You?

No, you are not crazy. The person you love is probably an alcoholic. In talking about my writing topic, I've met spouses, loved ones and family members who suspect that a person they love is an alcoholic. I consistently hear the phrase, "I think, no, I'm pretty sure he has a drinking problem."

Let me tell you this, if you are at the point in the game where you are questioning as to whether or not your loved one is an alcoholic, chances are extremely good that he or she is most definitely an alcoholic.

You see; denial is a big part of this disease. Denial comes not only from the person suffering from alcoholism himself but also from friends and family. Because of the stigma still attached to alcoholism, it's difficult to equate the person you love with the disease. It just doesn't seem possible. It's easier to find excuses and reason away any bad behavior associated with the drinking. When you have reached the point where the unacceptable has become acceptable, it's time to admit that the drinking is a problem. And by the time you are questioning as to whether or not he or she is an alcoholic, it is usually so far into the addiction that you have begun to accept the unacceptable.

Let me give you some examples. Is it normal for you to be the designated driver all the time? Can you not count on her to accomplish mundane tasks after 7 p.m. or on weekend nights? Is your loved one consistently making promises he cannot keep? When she's had a few drinks, does she argue with you or call you names? Does he get upset if you dare throw out a drink?

If you answered "yes" to any of these, you have begun or have been accepting the unacceptable.

But if you are still unsure, below is a list of signs of alcohol abuse.

A person who is addicted to alcohol:

- Drinks alone
- Hides alcohol in various places in the house or car
- Tries to control drinking (Non-alcoholics don't need to control drinking)
- Drinks excessive amounts at social gatherings when others don't drink as much
- Refuses to go to a venue for a social gathering where there is no alcohol
- Drinks in the morning
- Lies about drinking habits or tries to conceal it from family or friends
- Has had one or several DUIs
- Drinks alcohol fast for the effect
- Tries to "pregame" outings. Will drink a few drinks before going out for the night.
- Finds and makes excuses to drink
- Blames your actions or words as a drive to drink
- Avoids friends who don't drink
- Gets angry when confronted about drinking

- Changes personality and behavior when drinking
- Has blackouts or forgets what happened during a drinking episode
- Drinks even while taking prescription drugs
- Drinks to stave off the effects of a hangover
- Gets angry when someone throws away an alcoholic beverage
- Gets irritable, anxious or has the shakes in the morning after binge drinking the night before

In Al-Anon Family Groups, a support group for friends and family of alcoholics, a commonly used phrase is: *You did not cause his alcoholism. You cannot control his alcoholism. And you cannot cure his alcoholism.* Alcoholism is known as a social and family disease because the insanity of the illness infiltrates every aspect of life.

You Are a Good Person. And So Is Your Alcoholic.

If you are a family member, lover or friend of an alcoholic and reading this book, chances are you are a good person with good intentions. Remember, this disease is insane. It attacks the brain of the person you love and makes them crazy and irrational, but not all the time. As you will begin to understand by reading the stories in the following chapters, you are truly dealing with Dr. Jekyll and Mr. Hyde. But it's not completely their fault either, the person you love is very, very sick.

Many books on alcoholism give advice to stop enabling the alcoholic, and it's sound advice. However, I'm here to tell you that you should *never* feel guilty about anything you have done to help your alcoholic in the past. After all, being a good person, you would always help or lend a hand to anyone else in your life that needed help, right? People who enable or who are co-dependent, as many coin the term, are compassionate, empathetic people. People like you are caretakers. And there is *nothing* wrong with that.

Two Downfalls of Helping Your Alcoholic

Established in the fact that you are a compassionate, loving and empathetic person who finds it easy to care for others, try to understand the downfalls of helping your alcoholic.

Your alcoholic friend or family member has a disease that counts largely on consistently getting large amounts of alcohol and/or other drugs as the disease progresses. His emotional maturity stopped at the point at which he began abusing alcohol. His only goal is to get more alcohol to satisfy the drive within him. In doing so, he will neglect any and all responsibilities to cater to the drive to drink. This is where you come in.

The more you do for him, the less he has to do for himself and the more he can keep drinking and make himself sicker. So by doing more for him, you are actually prolonging the disease. He needs to experience consequences. He needs to stand on his own two feet. Yes, he's sick. But if you protect him, you are really protecting the alcohol, not him. Even though his brain function is severely modified, he has to somehow have that light bulb switch go on in his head that says, "Whoa, something is way out of control here." And that can only happen if he experiences all and every consequence of his drinking.

The second downfall is that you become so absorbed in what he is doing, that you forget yourself. The disease spins life so out of control; that any normal person would try to pick up the pieces and put it back together. However, as long as he's still drinking, you can't. No matter how hard you try, you can't. You need to take care of you. That is the best thing you can do for your alcoholic.

When I asked the question to my now alcoholic friends in recovery what advice they would give to family and friends, whose loved one is still drinking, they almost all answered unanimously, "Stop enabling." Here are ways in which you can stop enabling:

- Stop covering up his behavior.
- Do not give money to him ever, not even a dime.
- Tell her she cannot stay at your home until she gets help to get sober.
- Do not nag, plead or lay on guilt trips.
- Do not make excuses for her behavior.
- Do not call his work and give an excuse for why he is not there.
- Call the disease by name to other family members and friends. If you fear the word "alcoholic" has too much of a negative connotation, use "the disease of alcoholism" or "my loved one is addicted to alcohol"
- Do not believe his lies.
- Don't enter into an argument or a discussion when your loved one has been drinking.
- Do not undress her if she's passed out, clean up her vomit, move her into bed etc. Let her see and feel the consequences of passing out from drinking.
- Treat your alcoholic with respect. She is a human being who deserves your respect.
- Do not take any of his behavior personally. This is not about you. He has a disease. This is his own internal battle.
- Never accept physical or emotional abuse. Walk away and get out.
- Do set boundaries and keep them. If you say, "No!", keep it a "No!".

- Never join in on the alcohol party, even if she begs you. Your clear statement should be, "The alcohol is killing you. I love you too much to let this substance kill you." Even if this statement is non-verbal, let your actions show it.
- Do not buy him alcohol, drugs or any other substances.
- Get help with a psychotherapist who specializes in addiction and/or attend Al-Anon meetings.

Separating the Alcoholic from the Alcoholism

As a loved one of an alcoholic, you must, as much as you possibly can, separate the person from the disease. I understand that this feat is much easier said than done. Calling him bad, horrible, a demon or calling him every profane name in the book will not help. Making fun of her, shouting, or physically hurting her will not make her stop drinking. The disease is maddening because of its cunning nature. It appears at times, that you are dealing with a normal, functioning, rational person. Your alcoholic loved one may go to great lengths to make you believe he is normal and well functioning. And he is extremely convincing. The reason you have had such a difficult time separating the alcoholic from the disease of alcoholism is because you have frequent seemingly normal interactions with him. Then like a light switch, it flips and you are dealing with a whole different person.

In my case, Johnny was very good at concealing his alcohol use. He would binge drink liquor, with little odor, and would mix it with juice or an energy drink so you would only smell a fruity flavor on his breath initially. For months, this personality switch seemed completely random and happenstance. I had no idea it was alcohol induced. Then, all of the sudden, I was dealing with a moody, criticizing person when just five minutes before, he was rational and loving. It was at those times that I fell into the trap of thinking I was dealing with a normal person.

You Could Be Prince Charming or a Perfect Ten and It Wouldn't Matter.

You cannot be smart enough, beautiful enough, charming enough or giving enough to make your alcoholic stop drinking. You could be close to perfection and it wouldn't matter. Stop letting his affection for alcohol degrade your self-esteem. You cannot compete anyway. Remember that little green alien monster? It has completely taken over his brain.

The dopamine surge he gets from drinking is 10x what he would get from normal life's pleasures. All other life's experiences, including your love and affection, pale in comparison. The dopamine he gets from his brain is so low, because of the alcohol abuse; he is not able to feel pleasure like you can without alcohol or drugs.

Do you see that it was a losing battle from the beginning to believe that this is about you? It's about your loved one's illness and nothing more.

Expect That Your Alcoholic Will Be, Well, an Alcoholic.

Because there are moments of normality in the madness, we trick ourselves into thinking that he is miraculously normal again. That is why it is such a baffling disease. You can have a day, a week or a month when all appears normal. He's following through on promises. She's showing up to the kids' dance recital. He's bringing home a paycheck. Life seems peachy for a while. Then, boom, like that, it happens again. You come home to find him stumbling drunk and uttering nonsense. She calls you while she's behind the wheel and she's slurring her words. And you are shocked.

You shouldn't be shocked. Expect it. Unless your alcoholic is in recovery, he is *still* a drinking alcoholic. And alcoholics need alcohol to survive and their brain will tell them this always until complete recovery. Please do not be angry with him. Don't yell at her. Don't call him names and shout. An alcoholic drinks alcohol in excess. If you think otherwise, *you* are the crazy one.

I say that with the greatest amount of affection because we have all been there, including me. When my alcoholic would fall off the deep end, yet again, I would appear surprised, each time, for a long time. Until I realized that I was the crazy one.

Hope for the Hopeless

I have hope. I have hope. And when I feel weak, I have hope again. All we can have in this disease, for our loved one, is hope. Just like the alcoholic in recovery, we need to turn to our Higher Power for help.

In Al-Anon family groups, recovering family members follow the same 12-Steps that Alcoholics Anonymous follows. It's a powerful set of steps and calls on us to surrender to our Higher Power.

I am thankful for my experience with Johnny on a level I never imagined. Johnny's alcoholism has brought me closer to God. I had always thought I had a close relationship with my Creator. But I wasn't even close. The surrender and trust you *must* place in your Higher Power when you love an alcoholic is unmatched to most of life's experiences. It is harder than ever to love an alcoholic. I can attest to that. But your alcoholic spouse, son, daughter, brother, sister, mother, father, boyfriend, girlfriend, grandma, grandpa, or friend needs your unconditional love, prayers and understanding. You and God may be that person's only hope.

Actions Steps Once You Realize Your Loved One Is an Alcoholic

The realization that your loved one is an alcoholic can be a hard pill to swallow. Deep inside you may have known it all along. Now that you know what alcoholism is and what it does, your first impulse may be to try and fix it. As you read on, you'll begin to understand your role in your alcoholic's life and you will change your approach to the situation. For now, here are some action steps you can take.

1. Read step one in the 12 Steps of Al-Anon and Alcoholics Anonymous and acknowledge it.
   Step One: We admitted we were powerless over alcohol and that our lives had become unmanageable.
2. Find an Al-Anon meeting for yourself and an Alateen meeting for your teenagers. http://al-anon.org/
3. Get a therapist who specializes in addiction for yourself.
4. When your alcoholic is not under the influence of alcohol, calmly give facts about his behavior. For example, "When you start drinking, you become loud and critical." Giving him the facts is okay, placing blame or judgment is not.
5. Leave the room when she is inebriated.
6. Follow the steps in this chapter to stop enabling.
7. Surrender to your Higher Power.
8. Start telling the truth to family and friends who ask. You are now armed with a way to educate them that alcoholism is a disease. Simply stated you can tell them something like this, "I've always thought that (insert name) was just out of control and lacked willpower to stop after a few beers (or wine, vodka,

etc.). But I now realize that (he or she) has a disease and that without abstinence plus the proper help, (he or she) can't stop once (he or she) starts drinking. I'm working on changing my perspective and focusing on how I can change so that maybe (insert name) will want to change too."

Part One
Inside The Heart

The obscurities of addiction can make it difficult to get into the heart of an alcoholic. For many reasons, alcoholics are extremely guarded. In many cases, alcoholics, as children, had trauma and severely dysfunctional families. Most alcoholics are highly sensitive and feel deeply. Perhaps this personality trait makes it easier for them to fall prey to addiction because they have difficulty in dealing with these deep emotions.

Maybe you've tried, without success, to get emotionally close to your alcoholic loved one. The feelings they've buried and continue to bury with the drinking make it not only impossible for them to share, but also hard for you to understand and in turn, empathize with him or her.

While each person is different, we all experience the same array of human emotions. There is a similar pattern to the process of the disease of alcoholism that most alcoholics follow.

In the following chapters you will read the stories of many recovering alcoholics on different matters of the heart, mind and soul. If your alcoholic is still drinking, hopefully you will become enlightened to the inner workings of your loved one on every level. As you gain greater understanding, your empathy and compassion will increase. It's this increased compassion that will transform you and in your transformation, your perspective will change. With a changed perspective, your unconditional love will allow the space for your loved one to get better.

CHAPTER 3

Love

...And the greatest of these is love.
— 1 CORINTHIANS 13:13

Love is the most highly charged topic in any relationship but in a co-dependent alcoholic relationship it becomes an obsession. Is your alcoholic capable of love? Should you love him? Why can't she seem to love me like other people? In this chapter, I will attempt to demystify the world of love with an alcoholic.

Three Simple Yet Complex Words, "I Love You."

I've read many books and articles on the topic of alcoholism. I've followed blogs and online support groups. There is a school of thought out there that I simply do not believe and do not adhere to. Once I explain it, I'll let you make the choice as to what you believe.

A fear we all hold, on some level, is one, that "I'm not enough." And two, "Am I really worthy of love?" From the time we enter into this earthly plane, we are all striving to get the love we so desperately need. The bonds we have with our parents and caretakers give us this love or perhaps make us feel less love than we actually need. Most of us, much of the time, are seeking to receive the love we need and do what we can to get it.

Now infuse a relationship with an alcoholic into that scenario. The overwhelming story out there is that an alcoholic can't love you because he doesn't even love himself. While this may be partially true, I will prove to you that the above statement is not the entire picture.

On earth, we all come from brokenness. No one human alive today can love perfectly. As you grew up, your parents may have loved you. But there was, without a doubt, some hurt along the way, some pain and disappointments. Everyone experiences these things on some level. Or maybe you grew up in turmoil without a lot of expressions of love and perhaps you turned out O.K. and know how to give love. There are levels of love and levels of maturity in love. A baby's love is extremely conditional on having her basic needs met. She will love whoever provides for her. And you can have a 50-year-old adult, whose love is still conditional or you can have an eleven-year-old who seemingly loves unconditionally.

Your alcoholic was not always an alcoholic. He had a life before alcoholism. He had experiences of love, affection, compassion, and relationship. Even if he started drinking at age eleven, like one of the recovering alcoholics in this book, he had eleven years of parents, siblings, teachers, friends and family to show examples of love. I am going to take this one step further since recovery for you and your alcoholic includes your Higher Power. (For the sake of my writing, I will refer to my Higher Power as God. You can call your Higher Power whatever name you choose.) God is infinite love and infinite compassion. Your alcoholic came from this same creative Source of infinite love from whence you also came. Therefore, your alcoholic loved one has it in her to love you.

I mentioned in the previous chapter that an alcoholic stops maturing emotionally at the point at which she starts drinking excessively. That point could be at 10, 15, 21 or 30-years-old. In my experience, active alcohol addiction typically occurs well before age thirty. Our levels of experience give us the maturity of love. We love, learn, modify and love deeper, if we're healthy. Our capacity to love shifts from an infantile love of, "I love because you're providing for me," to a mature version of "I love because I am an expression of Divine love." Where you fall on that scale is dependent on a lot of factors, including your willingness to be vulnerable, authentic, truthful, and to draw your power to love from your infinite source, your Higher Power.

If your relationship with your alcoholic is one of great significance where love was developing in your formative years, such as in a parent-child relationship or in a committed love relationship, such as a marriage, your view of healthy love may get confused.

Your alcoholic loved one may say he loves you, and in his own way, he does. He genuinely does. Remember, he has the same capacity to love as the Source who created him. His love, however, may be an infantile-type love and in most cases, that is what it resembles. Let's go back to the initial lesson that your alcoholic has inside of her, a greedy, life-sucking, little alien green monster who has hijacked her brain into thinking that the *only* way she will live is to get and consume more alcohol. Every time your alcoholic tries to "be good" or tries to "please you", the brain hijacker says, "Get the alcohol first." So what ends up happening, is the conditional type of love you have seen and may continue to see in your alcoholic loved one's behavior. This love will look manipulative, self-serving, and conniving. For example, an alcoholic spouse may say to her husband, "I'll sleep with you if you go out and get me a bottle of vodka first." The non-alcoholic husband, who needs love just as much as the next person, caves under pressure and goes to buy the vodka in hopes of receiving love in return.

How Your Alcoholic May Not Have the Self Love That You Do

In life, we learn along the way that it's hard to give away that which you don't possess. If you don't have a lot of money, it will be difficult to lend a friend or family member $1,000. If you don't have a degree in medicine, you can't get a job as a physician. You can extend this logic to feelings, emotions, and desires. For example, if you have a hard time forgiving yourself, you will likely have a difficult time forgiving others. The same applies to love.

Your sense of self, self-worth and self-love comes in part by the love and connection feedback loop of your relationships. This feedback loop started with your parents and caretakers and extended to other family members, friends, and teachers. While conditional in a sense, this love and connection feedback loop works for most people. You do a good job and you receive love and praise. You perform a good deed or an act of kindness and the receiver showers you with appreciation, affection, or acknowledgement. You give affection and you receive it. Inside of you, this feedback loop tells you, "Hey, I'm a pretty good person. Look how others react to me and love me." And you feel good about yourself and your love quotient goes up with each feedback. The reason this tends to work is because we all have basic human emotional needs for love, connection, affection, appreciation, acknowledgment, and acceptance. When you are a part of a love feedback loop, you are receiving some or all of these basic emotional needs and you are also giving those in return.

There is however, a deeper more authentic type of love that comes from a connection to your Higher Power. You know you are loved and therefore you deserve love and can give love. If you haven't yet experienced this type of love, you will learn it in your recovery. Higher power love is the most authentic and genuine form of unconditional love you receive. Many people search their whole lives to experience this type of love and never achieve it because they're searching for it in human connection love.

Thus, no one's love giving or receiving is perfect, except for Divine love. However, we still have needs here, in earthly bodies, on this physical plane existence. So, the human love feedback loop tends to help us receive some of the love we need.

Your alcoholic loved one may have started out with this positive feedback loop in love and loving relationships. But as his disease progressed, his sense of self-love, self-worth, and his ability to love has diminished.

Let me illustrate. Your alcoholic does not understand what is happening to him. He is in denial that the actual problem is alcoholism. We are all, to some degree, self-critical and we tend to strive to do better, at least in some aspects of our lives. Your alcoholic is self-critical. He thinks it's a problem of control, willpower, or a life circumstance. He thinks that if only A, B, or C would change, he could control his drinking and it wouldn't be a problem any more. He has a hard time conceiving that alcoholism is a disease and that there is a little green alien monster controlling his brain. (Would anyone *really* agree to that reality?) So just like many of us, trying to achieve something or reach a goal, he tries and fails many times over. Well, when you try something and fail, time and time again, what happens to your self-esteem, self-worth, and self-love? First, you start to believe you are worthless, then you think there is something wrong with you, and finally, you start hating yourself for repeating the same mistakes over and over again.

Now, let's get back to the love and connection feedback loop. Already, your alcoholic loved one is feeling like a failure. He is admonishing himself for not being able to reach his goal of controlling his drinking. Next, enter you and other people in his life. You have not yet separated his alcoholic self from his true, authentic loving self and therefore have bundled his behavior all into one. (This is before you discovered he has a brain hijacker in his head.) He promised you, for the fifth time, that he would come home straight after work and take care of the kids so you could take your Zumba class at the gym. And yet again, he stopped by the bar to have a "couple of drinks" and lost track of the time. You are so infuriated that you go off on him, "You worthless, son of a *****! You never follow through on your promises. You're nothing but a drunk!" His love and connection feedback loop is reconfirming what he already has deducted about himself. To him, he *is* worthless. He *is* a drunk. He *is* an idiot for not being able to follow through once again. He will hear this from you and from his inner voice time and again. And his self-love will get smaller and smaller each time. How then, can you expect him to love at the same level that you're able to when his feedback loop is all messed up? He can't.

But She Loves the Alcohol...

Please don't mix up love with need. I too have fallen into this trap. I've gotten mean and sarcastic and turned into a person who I'm not by assuming that Johnny loved the alcohol but not me.

Your alcoholic doesn't love alcohol. She hates alcohol. But she desperately needs it. She may make jokes that she loves alcohol and that it's her only friend but she's lying. I have seen the agony in my loved one's face several times when I taunted him about his drinking.

Once day, when Johnny was supposed to be spending one month without drinking, I found out he was very drunk on vodka. I was irate that he had broken his promise to me. I said to him sarcastically, "Oh, you're just having so much fun with your booze." He looked at me sadly and said, "Fun, do you think this is fun? Do you think I'm having fun here?" It was at that moment that I realized how drinking wasn't a conscious choice for him.

Should I Love Him Then?

Loving an alcoholic is one of the hardest things to do. As a non-alcoholic, you go through much pain, have to endure crazy behavior, insults, lies, broken promises, inconsistencies, and shattered hope. Alcoholism turns your relationship and your world completely upside down. But the answer is, yes, you should love your alcoholic loved one.

You're not to love him because he deserves love. In truth, none of us really deserve love 100% of the time. You must love him because you are a loving human being and because your Creator loved you first. You are to love your alcoholic because love is the highest vibrational frequency that exists. To love is to raise *your* energy level and will help you heal.

Loving your alcoholic doesn't mean you can't love her from afar. If it is impossible or unbearable to be near her, send her loving thoughts, prayers and positive vibes. Let her know how much you love her and that you're praying she will get help soon.

Loving from I Corinthians 13:4-7[11]

This passage, so often read in wedding ceremonies, is one of the most profound statements of what a loving relationship should look like and how we should love. Having heard this passage many times, I have often glossed over the true meaning in these three simple versus.

---

11 *New Believers Bible Compact: First Steps for New Christians, New Living Translation,* (Tyndale House Publishers, Inc., 2010), page 1039, 1 Corinthians 13:4-7.

In my relationship with my alcoholic, I've turned to these versus for strength and a reminder of how to love. Below, I break down the verses as they apply to a relationship with an alcoholic loved one.

1. Love is patient and kind.

The love I have for my alcoholic loved one should be patient. His sobriety or lack thereof does not have to be on my timetable, but is up to him and God. I'm patient when he fails to stay sober or reaches for another drink because I know that this is *his* battle and not mine. In fact, my patience comes from knowing that he is extremely ill and is suffering inside. When I am impatient, I'm adding to his suffering. My impatience shows that I do not trust my Higher Power but am trying to control the outcome of the situation. I'm also patient with myself and acknowledge that I too am human and have shortcomings that might need to be changed.

2. Love is not jealous or boastful or proud or rude.

It's easy to be jealous of the alcohol. After all, it appears she's spending all of her time with the alcohol and not with you. If you are in a romantic relationship with an alcoholic, you might notice that he lets loose and starts flirting with other women while under the influence. He might even boast that he's having a good time and that his drinking buddies are more fun than you.

You may be jealous. But try to put things into perspective. Once your loved one is addicted to alcohol, she's not spending time with it by choice. It's because she has to. Certainly, it's her choice to take the first drink of the day, each and every time but once the alcohol is in her, she loses the ability to choose.

He might boast that he's having a good time or that his drinking buddies are more fun than you. Yet, here is the stark truth. He's not having fun. He's miserable on the inside. He feels trapped and all alone. He knows that his drinking buddies are not friends. Actively drinking alcoholics tend to use each other in many ways and that is not friendship.

You might be tempted to boast that you have it all under control. Comparing yourself to a person who is as lost and sick as an alcoholic is too easy. It can be tempting to have a self-righteous attitude when it comes to comparison. Of course it's easy for you to stay sober; you don't have the addiction. It's a given that you show up for meetings, dates, occasions and appointments because you are a normally functioning human being. Your alcoholic loved one is not.

Because she is so far off the deep end, it can feel easy to be rude to her. After all, she's *got* to pull it together. Since she doesn't appear to respect you, being rude to her may seem to be the only way to get through.

The slippery slope of jealousy, boastfulness and being rude is that it doesn't define the other person; it defines you.

3. It does not demand its own way.

Loving an alcoholic means that all of us have demanded our own way with him or her. You might not even have a recollection of being so demanding with another human being. Because of the nature of the disease, things seem out of control all of the time. It's natural to want some control and predictability in relationships and our environment. Setting boundaries and parameters for you is an absolute must. However, you will fail each time if you demand that your way be met with your alcoholic. Those of us who consistently demand that it's our way or the highway have weak boundaries to begin with.

The way to fix this problem is to make sure you learn how to and implement strong boundaries. For example, "I don't like it when you drink. Therefore, if you come over drunk or I suspect you've been drinking, you need to leave." That is an example of a strong boundary and it's only set if you follow through. An example of a demand is, "You cannot drink tonight." No one has control or really has the right to say how another person should behave.

Therefore, if you find yourself demanding your way with your alcoholic loved one, work on boundary setting.

4. It is not irritable and keeps no record of being wronged.

Who wouldn't be irritable with the mood shifts and the roller coaster ride of a drinking alcoholic? Yet, have there been times when your words, actions, and deeds caused irritability in another? Irritability is part and parcel of relationships in general. Irritability tends to come most when we think we can control the alcoholic's drinking or his behavior. The truth is we can't.

Often, when Johnny started to drink, he was feeling good. In the beginning, he would relax, his mood would improve and he would be the life of the party, so to speak. It was at that time, that I started to get more irritable. In my head I was thinking, *Oh no. Here we go again. It's just going to get worse. He's going to keep slamming down the vodka. And I won't even be able to have a decent conversation with him.* And I would get ornery, cranky, and irritable. Johnny, in response, would often roll his eyes at me. All he was doing is what he always did. He was, according to him, "having a good time". Meanwhile, I became a witch. Now if you look at the scenario from a distanced perspective, who was the crazy and miserable one? It wasn't him at that moment, clearly, it was me. I made myself miserable by reacting to something Johnny always did and would continue to do until he made the decision to get sober.

Keeping record of what the other person has done wrong is never a good idea in any relationship. But in an alcoholic/co-dependent relationship it's much worse. The alcoholic feels terrible about what he does. His guilt and shame are enormous. He truly does not understand why he can't control the drinking and why he can't behave like a normal person. The more you give him the laundry list of all the things he's done wrong, the more he sinks deeper into his own guilt. Another reason, it's destructive to keep record of his wrongdoings is that many things he did wrong were done under the influence. Most alcoholics experience blackouts, which means periods of time during which they don't remember anything. Chances are very high that he consistently doesn't even remember what he did, let alone be able to have accountability for his actions while inebriated. Lastly, it's highly likely that you've made wrong choices too, at some point. You would want the people with whom you are in a relationship to show mercy, compassion, and forgiveness toward you too, so you need to be ready to give it.

5. It does not rejoice about injustice but rejoices whenever the truth wins out.
In being a loving person, this is a difficult one to live out. Instead of making a blanket statement, I'm going to flip this one back onto myself. I believe this verse is about judgment. When you trust and believe in your Higher Power, you know that your Higher Power is the ultimate judge. No one handed you the scepter to make you the ultimate judge.

Yet, I am guilty of this. And I am especially guilty of this when it comes to my alcoholic loved one. I hope my alcoholic never reads this, but I used to pray and hope that he would get another DWI in order to spend a night in jail and get the wake up call he needed to get sober. I would pray that he would wind up in the hospital with just enough liver disease to push him to get help. If he would miss a day of work because of a nasty hangover, I'd get excited because I was counting that he was one day closer to sobriety. I was rejoicing in injustice.

It was never up to me or my prayers to make him hit rock bottom. My rejoicing in his potential misery was not rejoicing in the truth. Believing that I was the judge to determine when and how he would get sober, was denying the truth that God is in control of all.

Rejoice in the fact that you now know your loved one is suffering terribly from a nasty disease. Rejoice in the fact that it's not your fault and it's not your loved one's fault either. Rejoice in the truth that millions of alcoholics have recovered. Rejoice in the truth that you can recover too and live a happy, fulfilling life, whether your loved one continues to drink or not. In our own recovery, those are the truths we need to rejoice in.

6. Love never gives up, never loses faith is always hopeful and endures through every circumstance.

We live in a society where it's easy to give up. We are constantly changing and searching for something new and exciting. Many people today don't have the discipline and tenacity to stick through something difficult. If you truly love your alcoholic loved one, you will not give up on him or her. Marriage is hard. Relationships are challenging. Even if you have to live at a physical distance from your alcoholic, you can at least check in from time to time. You can always pray for him. You can extend your offer to her, "When you're ready to get into rehab, I'll be there for you."

While the situation may seem desperate and hopeless, you've been blessed with sobriety. As long as you have a relationship with your Higher Power, you can have hope. Hope simply means; I'm not big enough or powerful enough to see the grander picture, but I know my Higher Power is and he can see my loved one and I through this.

Love endures through every circumstance. Love is bigger than human error and human action. Committing to love comes from your spiritual self. You may be angry, upset, frustrated, fearful, hurt, or sad. Yet, you can continue to love because giving love is your ultimate goal. All love requires is an opening of your heart space. It lies in the knowing that you are not perfect and neither is your loved one. Love is not conditional on the moment; love is everlasting.

Action Steps to Giving and Receiving Love in an Alcoholic Relationship

1. Take Care of Yourself.

As a person who loves an alcoholic, you become as obsessed with her drinking as she is. When I was completely overtaken by the inner need to try to get Johnny to want help, I all but ignored my business, my finances and my friends. It is so easy to become totally absorbed with his stuff. *Here is a helpless man who can't get out of this trap*, you might tell yourself. *It's up to me to help him get out.* While that is a noble cause, it only becomes unhealthy when you spend so much time "helping" your alcoholic that you forget your needs and obligations.

Before takeoff, the flight attendants have a safety presentation where they urge you, in the case of loss of cabin pressure, to put on your oxygen mask before helping others. That is the idea in a relationship with an alcoholic.

Taking care of yourself means:

- Taking a shower and getting yourself dressed every day.
- Taking care of your needs first such as getting adequate sleep and eating properly.
- Getting exercise 3-5 times per week.
- Having friend time and maintaining healthy friendships.
- Getting to at least one Al-Anon meeting weekly and/or joining an online Al-Anon meeting.
- Setting healthy boundaries with your alcoholic and keeping those boundaries.

2. Treat Your Alcoholic the Way You Want to Be Treated.
Do you remember the Golden Rule? It is too easy to fall into the trap of lowering yourself to her level. Remember your alcoholic loved one is very sick. Once she has any alcohol in her body, it's the alcohol talking and not her. The best thing to do and the most loving thing to do is walk away. Try not to be sarcastic, make fun or call him names. Try not to get angry and raise your voice. I know how hard it is and how tempting it can be to lose it on him. It may make you feel better in the moment, but it will leave scars on both ends.

3. Forgive Your Loved One.
Forgive him for everything he does while drinking (or using any mind-altering substance) and ask for forgiveness when you do something wrong.

4. Forgive Yourself.
You are only doing the best you can at any given moment. Be aware of your actions, words and deeds but forgive yourself for past mistakes knowing that there is room to improve in the present and future.

5. Find Friends Who Fulfill Other Needs in Your Life
We all have the need for love and connection. It is healthy to have several people, in your life, who can fulfill different roles for you. If you have ignored other family relationships or friendships, take some time to renew your focus on those relationships while de-focusing on the relationship with your alcoholic loved one.

6. Learn About Safe People

If you have spent a lot of time being a people-pleaser, chances are you don't have a lot of safe people in your inner circle. Here are a few qualities of safe people:

- A safe person will accept you as you are.
- A safe person loves you no matter what.
- The influence of a safe person helps develop your ability to love.
- A safe person gives you the opportunity to grow.
- You can be yourself around a safe person.
- A safe person is honest, lives in truth and helps you to live in truth.

CHAPTER 4

How His or Her Relationship with Alcohol Began

*Alcohol doesn't console, it doesn't fill up anyone's
psychological gaps, all it replaces is the lack of God.*
— MARGUERITE DURAS

On an Al-Anon online thread, I once read the definition of an alcoholic put in simple layman's terms. *An alcoholic is someone whose primary relationship is with alcohol.*

It doesn't start that way, but that's the way it becomes. Alcohol becomes the trusted friend, the advisor, the go to for stress relief, and the only coping mechanism. To an active alcoholic, alcohol is reliable and faithful. This relationship fostered over years and often decades, has markers and milestones like most relationships.

Each person I interviewed remembers two events in his or her life distinctly, the first drink or drug and the day they became sober.

Tim, age 41, sober since October 27, 2008

I was swimming at a rock quarry. I was eleven years old. I was with some friends. My friend's best friend had a much older sister and they were there and gave us a lukewarm Budweiser. And

I remember it tasting horrible but I drank it all the way down because I didn't want to look like a fool in front of the older kids. I remember that for the longest time alcohol tasted horrible, but I drank it because it did something on the inside.

That same year we moved from South Carolina to Southern California and I would go and drink with a lot of the kids in the neighborhood and their parents would have full bars. At first it was just on weekends. But by the time I was fourteen; I was drinking every day.

The people I hung around with, at age fourteen, were all older than me. They taught me that if you can't do it drunk, you can't do it sober. And I learned to drive drinking. The first time I learned to drive, my friend got me a 12-pack and I learned to drive a stick.

I never saw alcohol or drugs in my house. My first drug problem was that I was "drugged" to church on Sunday. My stepfather didn't drink. He was a great man. But we lived in lower income neighborhoods and it surrounded us.

Raul, age 32, sober since September 5, 2011

I started using when I was 17 with pot. I remember it was January 1, 2001, the start of the millennium. I began to like getting high. I had a job and I didn't want it because I wanted the easy way, so I began selling pot. And at some point in that first year, I found alcohol. Honestly, I was always the type of kid that thought that kids that did alcohol and drugs were not good.

Rachel, age 45, sober since March 21, 2012

I had sips of alcohol at age thirteen. My mother would give me sips. I thought, "Oh, it's no big deal. It's just an Irish coffee."

Then, the summer I was about to turn fourteen, it was the end-of-the-year party, the parents were away and there were wine coolers and I remember it was a lot of fun. I was an uptight person, as a kid, and it made me feel loose, fun and flirtatious. Then I broke up with my boyfriend of many months for no reason and I cried and he said, "Where is this coming from?" It was then I realized that there were chemicals at work that really messed with my judgment. I was drunk. And the fun part of drinking transitioned into this hysterical crying.

I was fifteen and I remember going to Georgetown with my best friend, who was a couple of years older, and a couple of guys. We ordered a bunch of long island iced teas. I drank three of them, we left, and I threw up on the street. I had a fake ID and I just remember going out to the clubs.

Waldon, age 56, sober since March 31, 2009

I was probably about twelve or thirteen. My mother used to drink these Pabst Blue Ribbons in the basement. And my parents had a full bar. They weren't alcoholics but they liked to dance and have fun together. They were in the basement and I remember my mother had this grown up look when she was drinking the beer. When you're a little kid, there are deep impressions. I had a lot of emotional problems when I was a kid. I didn't know it at the time but I think I would have qualified as bipolar or manic-depressive. I remember trying the beer because I liked the grown up look my mother had on her face when she took a sip. When I took a drink the room started spinning and I felt dizzy. I liked it at first but when the room started spinning, I said to myself, I'll never do this again. But after that experience I would often sneak into the basement and take a beer and that's how it started.

Dan, age 47, sober since May 19, 2008

I was in the seventh grade. I was staying over a friend's house and he had stolen a six-pack from his dad. We were just kids in the summertime running around and I drank three warm beers in the bushes. From that moment on, it was what I chased. It became the reason for whom I hung out with, what school I went to, what relationships I had, and whatever lent to more drinking. I wasn't too impressed with the taste but it was the effect. I was going to be wild and crazy and have a good time. Right away we started figuring out how we could get more. My circle of friends were all spending the night at each other's houses and figuring out how we could get a couple of beers and go out vandalizing.

I grew up in a loving home. I never saw alcoholism anywhere. I later found out my grandfather's brother was a raging alcoholic.

Lee, age 53, sober since January 1, 2012

I grew up overseas. It wasn't uncommon for kids to have wine with soda over dinner. I remember those moments but I don't remember having my exact first drink, although I do remember being in grade school. I was introduced to alcohol very early and drinking was a part of our life. My first real diving into it, on my own, was around age thirteen. I was doing it to fit in. But from the get go I was a drug user. I came back to the U.S. around that time and all the kids who were nice to me were drinking and using drugs. What I do remember is that I liked it and I continued to do it by myself. I would go out and use or drink with friends, then I would go off by myself and do it alone.

Why Did the Drinking Start?

For someone who loves an alcoholic, it's difficult to understand the relationship process that their loved one has with alcohol. As you can see by these stories, sometimes there is a factor with an alcoholic parent and often there isn't. The genetic predisposition with alcoholism may skip a generation or may not even be apparent.

One thing is for certain; every alcohol addiction begins with a choice, the choice to have the first drink. In some cases, the choice to have the first drink comes before physical and emotional maturity, so the person doesn't have the cognitive ability to actually reason as an adult might. Either way, whether a person, who is predisposed to become addicted to alcohol, starts at age ten or at age twenty-one, there seems to be little difference in the outcome. The first drink inevitably leads to another on the same occasion or at another time.

There are several theories as to what caused the alcoholic to start drinking in the first place. Trauma may play a part. Personality traits might also be a factor. Environment or exposure to alcohol or drugs (i.e. from an alcoholic or drug addicted parent) in childhood can also contribute to accepting alcohol as a normal way of coping and therefore be more attractive as an option to start.

Personality Traits of an Alcoholic

Much research has been done on the pre-morbid[12] personality of an alcoholic. The conclusion among many is that the alcoholic personality prior to drinking is no different than non-drinkers with the exception of several exacerbated or exaggerated negative traits that seem to

---

12 The term *pre-morbid* here means before the alcoholic started drinking.

be present in most. Below are some of those traits the alcoholic seems to have more of in his or her personality.

1. Low frustration tolerance

Alcoholics have a low tolerance for discomfort, conflict, or when things don't seem to work out the way he or she wants. They tend to have more frequent or faster blowups of anger.

2. Impulsivity

During a healthy childhood, when given adequate choices and the opportunity to develop delayed gratification by making a conscious choice, you refine this skill into adulthood. Alcoholics tend to have a hard time delaying gratification. When they want something, they want it now.

3. High sensitivity

These individuals tend to be tuned in to others' energy and intensely sensitive to their own emotions. They are extremely perceptive and most are highly creative.

4. Low self-esteem

Prior to the obsessive drinking, many alcoholics say they were insecure, had low self-esteem and a low sense of self worth. I once heard a recovering alcoholic tell the story about growing up in an alcoholic home and that her parents constantly told her she was a bother, was worthless and that they wished she had never been born.

Tim

I used to drink like Captain Kirk would say, "As no man has ever gone before." I would get off work and drink as much as I could as fast as I could because I didn't want to remember, I wanted to be numb. There was anger and I used to say I hated everyone and everything but it was really hatred toward myself. It was a low self-esteem thing.

Raul

Since I can remember, there was a lot of internal dialogue and a lot of not being present. There was a lot of judging myself, a lot of caring about what other people thought. My insides didn't match what other people's outsides did and when I started using, whoa, all that went away.

5. Loners

Many alcoholics are not joiners. They feel they don't fit into a group or mold. Even if they weren't loners before excessive drinking, the progression of the disease of alcohol causes the alcoholic to isolate himself. That is the main reason why rehab centers often have recovering alcoholic stay in a room with roommates and why all recovering alcoholics are encouraged to not only do individual therapy sessions but to have their main focus of recovery on a daily 12-Step group meeting.

6. Perfectionism

Alcoholics tend to want things to be perfect the first time. They also see the world completely in black and white. According to them, there is a right way and a wrong way to do things.

7. High anxiety/ Fear

As you might imagine, many of these personality traits, exaggerated, interplay with each other. A person with low self-esteem, high sensitivity and who has a low frustration tolerance will also experience high anxiety. The inner dialogue, that plays, go something like this, "I'm not good enough, strong enough, good looking, or talented. People don't like me and I am unworthy." Playing these recordings over and over in your head would give you high anxiety too.

Certain alcoholics have what medical professionals call *dual diagnosis*. An alcoholic can have a pre-morbid diagnosis of clinical anxiety, depression, bipolar disorder, or psychosis. However, many alcoholics self medicate with alcohol before they are actually diagnosed. The side effects from excessive and prolonged drinking can also cause mental illness to form. Therefore, it can be difficult for a medical practitioner to know if the mental disease existed before the addiction or was formed as a result of the addiction.

8. Egocentricity

We all can be, at times, egocentric. But for the alcoholic, he suffers from it at all times. Egocentricity says, "I am the center of the universe and I need to get what I need at the expense of everything and everyone else." The person with extreme egocentricity believes he is the sun, the center of the solar system, and that everything else revolves around him. (And in an alcoholic/ co-dependent relationship, that is typically what happens.) For better and for worse, the entire universe is for or against him. The alcoholic probably had a pretty strong sense of egocentricity before he started to drink, but that character defect grew worse as he delved deeper into the disease. Egocentricity says:

- People are talking about me.
- People are out to get me.
- I am entitled to that.
- You forced me to do that.
- I deserve that.
- You have the problem, not me.

Egocentricity is a child-like state. It is a state in which the ego rules all, much like a two-year-old child who believes the world revolves around her. The arrogance and self-centeredness, that plague alcoholism and alcoholic relationships, does not mean the person perceives that she is superior in any way. It outlines the deep-seated insecurity and low self-esteem underlying the demands, arrogance, and blame.

The Point of No Return

Every alcoholic experiences a moment in time when he or she has some realization that drinking is no longer a choice but that it's become an obsession or compulsion. Even if your loved one doesn't admit she's an alcoholic or has delusions about the problem, she's quite aware that a line has been crossed somewhere.

Tim

In my 20s I knew that this is what's killing me and saving me all at once and I don't know how to stop it. I can't stop the cycle. It's the only thing that's keeping me mentally capacitated to handle people and at the same time it's pushing me away from every person I ever met. Because who wants to be around Tim the drunk.

I went to a 28-day rehab and didn't do well. I learned a lot. I learned how to hide it a little bit better. The disease is a mental disease and it's so overwhelming. I couldn't wrap my head around having a Higher Power. That was just too much for me.

After rehab I went back to bartending. And I thought, *This is the stupidest thing in the world, I can't be a sober bartender. Sober bartenders are boring.* I started drinking and it came back faster after rehab and it was more aggressive. But it was always aggressive with me.

Rachel

I was binge drinking. And then I would go four to five days and live like a normal person. Then, I would go and sleep with a person I swore I would never sleep with. I had an active eating disorder from age fourteen to twenty-one. But when you have an addiction, you better watch out because the addiction will shift. So I had worked the 12 Steps previously in Overeaters Anonymous (OA). So after I slept with this guy, I went to an OA meeting and it was one of the ladies at the meeting who said to me, "You should go to AA because you reek of vodka." I got three months sober and then, I felt it was safe to drink again and that was over ten years ago. So it took all that extra time to actually get sober.

Waldon

I ended up in detox at about fourteen-years-old. When I was upset, that was my outlet. I would go out with this older kid down the street from me. Turned out he was a heroin addict. We didn't have drugs per se in my neighborhood so I don't know where he got his drugs. I would take beer from the house to go hang out with him. I think I helped my father stop drinking altogether because I would take all of his beer and liquor.

I remember going out and there was this "wino" guy who asked my friends and I to carry cases of beer to his house because he and his friends were too drunk to carry it. They were playing pool and started gambling. They gave us these ponies to drink (little 8-oz beers) and we ran out. Then there was a tall bottle and I started going toward that. I think it was vodka. I left and passed out in front of someone's door. My parents sent me to detox and I don't remember much of it. A lot of it was a blackout. I just remember a doctor telling my mother that I was going to have to learn by the school of "hard knocks". I think it was at that time, that I was gone.

Shortly thereafter I saw this movie, called "Portrait of a Teenage Alcoholic" with Linda Blair. And I wanted to be an alcoholic because she got a lot of attention from her family. I knew I wanted a lot of attention.

Dan

I don't remember the point of no return. That's the invisible line we cross. I would always tell myself, "I'm probably drinking too much and I can stop anytime I'd like, but I don't want to." I was in my 20s and drinking six beers a night. I would find the friends who were hanging out that night and drink the beers. I would get up in the morning, and do what I needed to do.

I came to a point where I'd try to control it and try to take breaks from it and I couldn't, I had crossed that line. I didn't have a choice at that point. That was in my 30s. It was funny how it progressed because my intentions were always to slow down. I would say, "When I get married, I'll slow down." But it escalated. I had my first child and I thought that would slow me down. First child came and went, the drinking increased. It was getting worse and worse and I couldn't figure out why. I kept putting these lines in the sand and saying, "I gotta grow up. I need to start buckling down." I knew it was affecting my health too. Not only was it eating my soul, but my body, I could feel it killing me. I was not an all- around-the-clock drinker; I was a daily binge drinker. I would start drinking at 4:30 or 5 p.m. whenever I got off work.

I would get up in the morning feeling like crap and make myself sit at work all day long. All I could think about was getting my next drink. And then I would leave the office and go to the closest convenience store and get an 18-pack of beer and a 24-ouncer to drink on the way home. I would drink that through a straw in a paper bag and right then I could start breathing again. I could relax.

Lee

I had a fear of vomiting so I gravitated more toward drugs than alcohol in the beginning. When I met my first husband at age twenty-five, who was an active alcoholic, I discovered how well I could hold my alcohol. But I was comparing myself to him and he could drink two fifths of hard liquor per day. It seemed that what I was doing in comparison was negligible.

At one point we went to marriage counseling because of him and we each had to take an alcoholism questionnaire test. I remember clearly that he failed the test and that I passed the test. He ended up going to treatment at a certain point. Fast-forward several years later to me going to AA. I'm about a year into recovery and I went back to talk with that therapist that we had gone to all those years ago. I said, "It's just odd that we didn't think I was an alcoholic back then." The therapist went and found my file and found the alcohol test that I took and I had failed it too.

Action Steps to Examine Personality Traits That Might Affect Relationship

Everyone has experienced or does experience at least some of the flaws outlined in the alcoholic personality traits. Read them over and get honest with yourself. You might find that you do, in fact, share a lot of these traits with your alcoholic loved one. There are different sides of relationship regarding these traits and your alcoholic relationship. If you are an Adult Child of an Alcoholic (ACOA), you likely developed some of these traits because you grew up in an alcoholic household where there was a lot of uncertainty, loads of insecurity, and lack of trust in the foundation of a relationship. If you didn't come from an alcoholic household, but fell in love with an alcoholic or have a son or daughter who is an alcoholic, your personality traits may be different or may have been exacerbated toward the negative side as the relationship with your alcoholic loved one has progressed.

Let's take the example of fear or high anxiety. As an ACOA, you grew up with a lot of fear because you never knew if your alcoholic parent would be there, follow through, or be sober enough to take care of you. You maybe had fear because you experienced violence, physical or emotional, and you had to deal with a Dr. Jekyll and Mr. Hyde personality. If you are a person, who was an adult upon entering into a relationship with an alcoholic, you may have already been an anxious person or you may have developed worries, anxieties and fear because of the unpredictability of an alcoholic relationship.

As you can see, even if you didn't have many of these personality traits from the beginning of the relationship, some of them most certainly developed in time as a result of the relationship.

I will share my example of becoming a loner. I became so absorbed with my alcoholic loved one that I put all of my focus on him and trying to get him into recovery. I spent a lot of time trying to convince him, giving him positive reinforcement (and sometimes negative reinforcement), and making sure he was where he said he would be. Therefore, I allowed all of my free time to be taken up by him and his disease. Furthermore, I felt embarrassed because I knew if I accepted social invitations and took Johnny with me, that there would be some sort of disaster. So I stayed away or went alone. I stopped developing friendships. I stopped networking. Toward the end, I became a loner just like my alcoholic loved one.

By becoming aware of these traits within you, you'll be able to heal them or bring them back to a more normal and acceptable size.

1. Look at the list above and get honest with yourself about which traits you have in an exaggerated form.
2. If you had a magic wand and could poof away one trait from your life, what would it be?
3. Do you expect more from your alcoholic loved one than you expect from yourself? (For example, you expect her to be honest but you justify your own lying. Or, you expect him to behave perfectly every time, but don't behave perfectly yourself.)
4. What is one trait you can focus on improving this week?

CHAPTER 5
Trust

Trust is the first step to love.
—*MUNSHI PREMCHAND*

Accarding to psychologist, Erik Erickson, trust is formed during the first two years of life. If the care we receive in those first two years is reliable, consistent and predictable, we develop a sense of trust, which leads to the virtue of hope. In the event that our early care was harsh, inconsistent, unpredictable, and unreliable, we grow into mistrust, which forms a sense of fear. Children growing up in the latter environment do not feel the world is a safe place. Sixty percent of alcoholics grew up in alcoholic households where the sense of trust was not well developed in childhood. An alcoholic household is unpredictable and chaotic with little to no healthy boundaries. Other alcoholics developed a great sense of trust, in a healthy home environment, as they grew up. However, once the seeds of addiction took root, their sense of trust in themselves was shattered.

Because of the inconsistency in behavior with a drinking alcoholic, trust or lack thereof is a major problem in relationships.

In my relationship with Johnny, I became suspicious of everything. I was always a person who trusted others. In fact, I was often naïve and too trusting. I took what people said at face value and believed they were telling the truth. When Johnny said he wouldn't drink and drive, I trusted him. If he made a promise to not bring alcohol in my house, I believed every word. But then, after being burned so many times, I learned not to trust. It got so bad that when he was telling the truth or following through, I was still suspicious. Then my behavior became insane. I was checking up on him constantly. I would drive to his house to see if his car was there. If a text came in on his phone, I would run to check it before he did. It was awful and tiring.

Trust makes us feel safe. Trust is consistency and security. Trust says, "I am there for you." Yet, your alcoholic can't be there for you when she can't even be there for herself.

Trust Issues from the Trenches

Many recovering alcoholics have trust issues from childhood. Growing up in dysfunctional or alcoholic homes hinders the sense of trust in adulthood. Not trusting others in relationship often results in self-fulfilling prophecies as many alcoholics choose toxic relationships. For the alcoholic, as the disease progresses, he learns not to trust himself and that is perhaps the scariest lack of trust of all.

Tim

We had a lot of problems at home. We went from being a middle-class family to being homeless and living in a car. I was a teenager and just about to get my driver's license. And instead of being that person to go out and get a job and help, I got a job so I could buy more alcohol and drugs. It really became an anger issue with me. I used to say to my parents, "If you can't pay your own bills, you can't tell me what to do." And my mom had cancer at the time too. They were going bankrupt and my mom had cancer. I was just angry about the whole situation. Every time I came home, something of mine was gone because they sold it to pay a bill.

When it came to trusting myself, I knew I couldn't trust myself. I'm very trusting of people. I try to think of a better side of humanity. I couldn't trust myself. I remember being twenty-five and twenty-six and saying to myself, "I can't drink like this all the time and tomorrow I'm not going to drink. I'm not going to have one drink. I know I'm not going to have one drink." And then tomorrow would come and I would have a drink. And I would be like, "O.K. so I can't quit on a Wednesday. I have to quit on a Monday. So I'm going to go through until Sunday and then Monday morning I'm going to get up in the morning and I'm going to do the right thing." And the right thing to me was like getting up and going to the gym or going to the beach and going surfing, not having a drink and just having a normal diet. And it just never happened. As soon as I got that one drink in me, it was off to the races.

Rachel

I didn't know my father. We left from Spokane, Washington so my mother could study music here in D.C. And the message that came was, "Men are not necessary. Relationships don't matter. Family is secondary to my dream. And so are you, Rachel, by the way." And that was my mother. So at five-years-old we came here. I turned six in a U-Haul driving from Washington. I didn't understand we were never going back and I didn't understand that I was never going to have my grandma. My mom didn't want me to know my father because he was a Jehovah's Witness and she was afraid. So when I look at all that, I was angry with her, furious, consciously and unconsciously. And so I couldn't even bring myself to confide in her when I was hurt or when I was sad. I just stopped feeling. So looking at that, you know there are going to be problems later on.

I think I wanted to not need anybody. I wanted to never feel the possibility that someone could let me down or disappoint me.

I couldn't trust myself because I lied to myself again and again. It's terrible. Letting myself down was terrible. In the end there was drinking every day.

Raul

I grew up in a great household. My parents loved me. I could trust them. There was one occasion with my mom, who was my confidant, and it only happened once but I told her something and she said, "That's why your friends don't like you!" But I was a brat and I must have done something bad to make her react like that.

In the midst of alcoholism, trusting or not trusting myself didn't even cross my mind. I didn't even really know what alcoholism was. But in sobriety, yes, trusting myself has crossed my mind. Before sobriety, I gambled maybe four times. In sobriety, I was gambling four times per week. I was trying to substitute. I was trying to fill this thing inside of me to make me feel whole. Nothing of this material world is going to do that. And I couldn't trust myself. It's been several months since I've done it, but I had to come to crushing lows with that.

Dan

Not trusting myself was an issue. Being at home with the kids, my wife would go out of town on a business trip and it was just the kids and I. I would try not to drink too much. They wouldn't fall asleep and I would have them on the couch with me as I was getting drunker and drunker. They were one and three-years-old. Finally, I would have to take them to bed and I could hardly stand up straight. I had to pick them up and take them upstairs. There was a big open foyer with the stairs and I had to lean on the wall as I was walking up the stairs because I was afraid of falling or dropping one of them over the banister. I remember thinking to myself, *What if something happens to them tonight. What if one of them falls and breaks an arm? I can't take care of them.* I didn't trust myself and the guilt and shame of just being a failure as a human being, not much less a father. It was heartbreaking.

Lee

I've never been one to really trust men. I'm definitely an Adult Child of an Alcoholic filled with trauma. My mother was the alcoholic. She's been a dry drunk for twenty-one years. I think I was looking for love and acceptance in all the wrong places and I was so desperately seeking that from a man. I was so afraid I was going to lose that and so I didn't trust because I was never in a normal relationship. I was in the wrong relationships for the wrong reasons with the wrong people who couldn't be trusted because they weren't trustworthy. And then I became the non-trustworthy person later on in life.

Action Steps to Foster Trust in Healthy Relationships

Below are some suggestions on how you can be trustworthy and what to look for in someone you can trust. The buzzwords of trustworthy relationships are in parentheses.

1. Faithfulness (Integrity and Honesty)

Being faithful in romantic relationships means you are upholding the integrity of your relationship on a physical, emotional, and psychological level. Faithfulness in other relationships includes keeping the other person's private conversations with you private, respecting the other person's wishes and desires, and holding the relationship at a place of importance.

2. Allow the other person space and show kindness. (Freedom)

No one likes to feel imprisoned in a relationship. Your loved one should be free to live her life without having you interfere. I like to refer to this interference as micromanaging. Even children need space to explore and make their own mistakes. And when she does make a mistake, refrain from admonishing, shaming, or saying, "I told you so."

As co-dependents or enablers, we love to micromanage. It's especially important in your relationship with your alcoholic loved one that you let him make his own mistakes, fall on his own butt, and pick himself up off the floor every single time with all choices.

3. Love the person for him or herself and not for what that person brings to the table. (Acceptance)

Try not to have a hidden agenda in your relationships. Even trying to "fix" someone is a hidden agenda. First and foremost, love him for who he is. Accept him for his talents and faults.

4. Create time for your relationship. (Prioritize)
Trust is built in the knowing that, "You are important to me." And importance is created through time spent together.

5. Stick through different emotions, stages and experiences. (Stability)
Everybody has bad days, bad years and horrible experiences in life. Sticking through the tough times will bring you better ones. In your alcoholic relationship, sticking through tough times can even mean accepting physical distance until your loved one is ready to accept help. Stick-to-itiveness does not mean you're a doormat. It simply means you don't threaten to leave or throw in the towel at every turn.

6. Be reliable. Honor appointments, show up for your commitments, and give notice if you need to change. (Reliability and Consistency)
It goes back to consistency, honorability, and integrity, the building blocks of trust. In your relationship with your alcoholic loved one, you have endured lack of reliability probably close to a million times, right? However, your behavior is based on your integrity and self-worth. You are holding yourself to a higher standard for you and you alone.

7. Be truthful. (Authenticity and Vulnerability)
We all know that outright lying is wrong. However, being truthful is more than that. It's not sugarcoating things or beating around the bush. Trust is developed with sincerity, openness, and vulnerability.

8. Share feelings. (Openness)

When something hurts, say it. When you're bursting with love, tell the other. Take away fears that are holding you back from sharing. And as one of my guru's, Dr. Wayne Dyer, used to say, "What you think of me is none of my business." Even though you may share your true feelings with someone, those are *your* feelings. And how others react doesn't matter.

9. Set boundaries. (Healthy Limits)

Relationships with no boundaries are scary places to explore. Boundaries say, "This is where my white picket fence is and that is where yours is." Healthy boundaries help us delineate responsibilities and keep privacy.

For example, it's acceptable to say, "no" in a relationship. I once learned that, "No," is a complete sentence, no further explanation required. In the book, *Boundaries* by Dr. Henry Cloud and John Townsend, they teach that it's not the end of the world if your healthy boundary hurts someone as long as it's not harming them. For example, saying to your alcoholic daughter, "You may not live with me until you go to rehab," might hurt her but it's not harming her.

10. Have faith.

Have faith that your loved one will do the right thing. Try not to see the glass as half empty and that the person will somehow mess up. Since many of us have been beaten down by co-dependent relationships, our tendency is to see the sky falling.

In early sobriety, Johnny asked me to have faith in him that he was attending his AA meetings. But I couldn't have faith in him because the trust was gone. So I had to have faith in my Higher Power that He would lead Johnny to meetings. Your Higher Power is greater, stronger, and more powerful than you can imagine. And if you ask, He can help you have faith in all of your relationships.

CHAPTER 6
Loneliness & Isolation

Loneliness is the poverty of self;
Solitude is the richness of self.
—MAY SARTON

Too much self-centered attitude, you see, brings
isolation. Result: loneliness, fear, anger. The extreme
self-centered attitude is the source of suffering.
- DALAI LAMA

The deep pit of loneliness and despair tortures the alcoholic in his intermittent moments of sobriety. It happens when he doesn't have enough alcohol to drink, when he has to go to work, or at any time he must abstain from drinking. Imagine what goes on inside of him. He begins to see that he's drinking more and more and that it's actually taking up most of his time. He feels the obsession to get the next drink. Alcohol infiltrates every one of his thoughts. When he summons up the willpower to try and stop, the addiction takes over and he doesn't understand why. He is so embarrassed that he cannot share with anyone because he's ashamed of being so out of control. He is in a deep pit and doesn't know how to get out. Even though he's often with other people who drink, he understands that he is not like most people. This creates an even deeper rift between him and others. Then there are his family members. They are angry and upset most of the time. He doesn't have the clarity to explain to them what's going on so he isolates himself even more.

The loneliness that you feel as someone who loves an alcoholic is real too. I cannot begin to count the lonely nights going out or watching TV by myself because Johnny was too drunk or passed out to participate. I felt deep loneliness because I wanted to share my innermost thoughts and feelings but his state made him self-absorbed and unable to process. I think the biggest aspect of loneliness I felt was in the knowing that we weren't creating memories together. I had one reality; a sober one and he had another reality, through the eyes of alcohol. And even though we were at the movies, at a nice restaurant, or on vacation, I knew our memories weren't even close to being the same. That brought about a great feeling of isolation and loneliness.

Alcoholic Loneliness & Isolation from the Trenches

The secretive nature of alcoholism brings about loneliness and isolation. Try to not be fooled when your alcoholic loved one says he's having so much fun with his friends. He's not. He feels lonely, isolated and disconnected. Do you know the expression *Misery loves company?* That's all it is. Alcoholics bunch together to drink in their isolated misery. The progression of alcoholism leads to greater amounts of time spent alone. The alcoholic is embarrassed by the quantity she drinks and prefers to hide out rather than have others notice. The behaviors that accompany alcoholism cause family members and friends to not want to be around the alcoholic. I'm sure you've experienced this. The name-calling, fights, lies, and manipulation, not to mention the embarrassing behavior has probably led you to leave your alcoholic loved one in many situations. Yet, as lonely as it is to be caught up in the drinking, many alcoholics have a hard time finding a way out.

The alcohol, which causes the loneliness and isolation, is also a crutch used to forget.

Tim

I had quite a few relationships where an ultimatum came up and I was like, "Goodbye." Alcohol wins. Consequences never worked for me.

Another reason I drank to pass out was to not realize how lonely I was. What really came hard for me was, every once in a while, there'd be nights when I didn't have enough money to drink the way I wanted to. I'm sitting in my apartment and there's no one to call because no one really wants to hang out with you. At the end, no one hung out with me. I had no friends whatsoever. And no one in my family really talked to me either, even my mother who was the most supportive. I lived ten minutes from her at the end because I went homeless in San Diego from my drinking and I couldn't get another job. I lived in a park and there were times when I went five days without ever talking to another human being. I would just drink out of my brown paper bag. It plays tricks on you.

There were times when I was sitting in a full bar with two hundred people around me and I never felt more lonely. I was just so lonely, constantly lonely all the time. Because I knew I was just stuck in that bottle.

Raul

Yes, I felt lonely and it felt like, "You better find some alcohol and drugs quick." It was just empty inside. And that still happens. I was at the World Conference for Alcoholics Anonymous with over 100,000 alcoholics and there was a moment, during some lunch hour, when I had broken apart from my friends. There was just a lot going on. And to feel the alcoholic loneliness, in the middle of 100,000 alcoholics...It's usually because I'm thinking about myself. On some level, it's maybe a self-centered thought. It's lack of faith. Because I'll have moments on the other side where I know I'm never alone. And I can feel that. But I'll tell you what, I start building those cases and I feel alone and the world isn't my oyster. You miss human contact. You miss human connection. Your Higher Power feels so far away. It happens a lot. I know people twelve years sober who kill themselves because of that issue. AA has a good course of action for that though, "Go help someone else."

Waldon

Loneliness was a good excuse to drink because it felt good when you're depressed. You hear people listening to the blues or country western, and when you're drinking it feels so good. I felt good feeling bad.

You feel that internal struggle when you wake up in the morning and realize that you're not working or that you're about to lose another apartment. My drinking took everything away. They say it's like a paint stripper. My friend use to say, "I'm a social drinker." When anybody would drink, I would say, "So shall I." That was his definition of "social drinker" and that described me.

You get to the point where you really want to stop but realize that you can't and that you're trapped in it. There is another expression that goes, "The man takes a drink. The drink takes a drink and the drink takes the man." Once you take it, you don't know when to stop.

Dan

I would just come home from work and go down into the basement to drink. I was very isolated. If I went to a party I would have a couple of drinks before just to feel comfortable. Then I would only have a couple at the party and go home early so I could go drink as much as I wanted. As for my wife, I would stop talking to her at 9 o'clock because, first of all, I didn't want her to hear me slur and second of all I didn't want to have a conversation with her that I didn't remember the next morning.

The loneliness is not just loneliness like there is nobody to talk to. It's loneliness with yourself and the remorse of the past and the fears of the future and there is no spiritual connection to anything. I felt like I was alone on this planet. It does cut you off from everyone because you're too afraid to get away from drinking the way you want to drink to go out to a ball game, for example. I chose drinking over everything and that makes it very lonely. It's sitting on the couch every night watching TV and drinking eighteen beers. In your head you're saying, "You know you're never going to do anything. You're a piece of shit and your life sucks and it's never going to change."

Lee

The last year I didn't go out much. I didn't want to go anywhere and did most of my drinking at home. I didn't feel isolated from people. But I knew I was different and I knew I was hiding a dark secret. I remember seeing a guy mowing his lawn and saying to myself, "Wow! I envy him because he's living such a normal life and I'm living such a shit life." I felt so disconnected.

There was a woman I worked with who lived in Chicago and we would get on a call at night to talk about work. I knew she was drinking. But she was always bright and bubbly and she'd get so much done. She would whip out four Power Points during the night and she would be up early the next day. And I was passed out at night after the call and I couldn't get up in the morning. I was hung-over and couldn't figure out how to do a Power Point much less create one. So I felt very different from everybody. I was isolated in front of everybody.

I was up at a podium talking about this company and everybody was clapping and thinking I'm amazing and I'm feeling like a big fraud and a failure. I'm thinking, "I really suck and one day they'll figure it out."

Action Steps to Help You Get Out of Loneliness and Isolation

1. Pull Yourself Out of the Victim Mindset.

"Why is she doing this to me after all I've done for her?" "I see others with a happy marriage, why is mine so horrible?" We have all been there. We see life as happening to us rather than us happening to life.

When you find yourself in self-pity mode, realize how powerful you are. Write down all of your gifts and talents and see how wonderful you are and how many contributions you can give to the world.

2. Go Help Someone Else.

Take your gifts and talents and go serve somewhere. Help a friend de-clutter a closet, take your neighbor's dog out for a walk, make dinner for a mom with a new baby or volunteer at an animal shelter. Helping others (outside of your own family) allows you to expand your vision of reality.

3. Go to an Al-Anon Meeting.

No one understands your situation better than others who have lived in your shoes. I'm not preaching that Al-Anon is a utopia, far from it. However, the program, which is similar to Alcoholics Anonymous, works. And every person attending has lived with alcoholism or an alcoholic loved one. Meetings are free with an optional donation of a dollar or two.

4. Get on Your Knees and Pray.
You may feel lonely but you are never alone. Your Higher Power is omnipresent, all loving, compassionate and caring. Prayer and surrender are two ways to snuff out the loneliness. If you don't have a relationship with your Higher Power, see the bullet point above, get to an Al-Anon meeting and the program will teach you how.

5. Explore the Real Reasons Why You Feel Lonely and Isolated.
It's good sometimes to explore the source of your loneliness. What's going on? Is there an emotion you're trying to avoid? Have you been procrastinating on completing a task? Have you isolated yourself because you've been too worried about your alcoholic loved one?

6. Play.
Do you have children, grandchildren or a pet? Can you babysit someone's child? Play is best seen through the eyes of a child or animal. Even watching play will help you feel more connected. Grab a friend and play tennis, kick around a ball with your kids, color; there are a many different ways to engage in play.

7. Be Grateful.
One of the first things I read about alcoholism is, "Be grateful every day that you are blessed with the gift of sobriety." In your alcoholic household or relationship, that is the simplest and most important thing to be grateful for. Gratitude keeps you in an abundant mindset. Gratitude brings about hope that things can and do get better. Hope is connection. Despair is disconnection. Even if your alcoholic loved one gave you one smile today, be grateful for that.

Part Two
Inside The Mind

Much of what goes on inside the mind of an alcoholic is hidden from view. Alcoholics are adept at morphing into their environment, in other words, being what you want them to be. They have learned, from practice, that if they want to continue drinking at all costs, they have to play the game of life to the extent that people think they are playing along.

For example, you might notice that after a particularly bad episode, your alcoholic loved one is sweet, kind, attentive and loving. In your head, you think, "Oh, she finally learned her lesson. She's back to normal now. I'm so glad." You might even tell friends and family how good she's acting. Yet, on the inside, her mind is already planning the next drink or binge. She does just enough to get you off her back so she can give in to the obsession that rules her every thought.

Her mind does not work like yours or mine. Until she gets sober, she will never share with you what's truly there. Let's explore what goes on in the mind of an alcoholic.

CHAPTER 7

Denial & Disillusionment

Denial Ain't Just a River in Egypt
- Mark Twain.

The most maddening aspect of the disease of alcoholism is the denial that runs rampant through it. The alcoholic is in denial that he has a problem or that it is a disease. Loved ones are in denial that the drinking is as bad as it is. Extended family or outsiders are in denial that alcoholism could possibly even be a disease because it's certainly a "lack of willpower" or a "personality flaw" and if she could just get herself under control, it wouldn't be a problem.

Denial's partner and friend is disillusionment. Even though nothing has changed, the alcoholic is certain that it will be better next time. He can control the drinking. He will look for that new job. As a loved one you may begin overlooking the obvious and painful consequences of the drinking and fantasize about him staying sober for the picnic over the weekend, even though he's never done it before. Disillusionment is when you believe her when she convinces you that her plan is to stop drinking on Monday and she's signing up for yoga, meditation, boot camp, and will go on a juice fast.

Denial comes as accepted lower standards such as, "Oh, at least he didn't throw up at the children's basketball game." Or "She may assign me as the designated driver every time, but at least she's not driving drunk." These kinds of denial lead us to our own disillusionment about our needs, wants, and desires. It also distorts our reality of what is normal and acceptable and what isn't. Is there any normality in a father not throwing up because he's too drunk at his son's basketball game? Or, is there normality in you having to drive all the time because your spouse, brother, sister, mother or father is always too drunk to drive? There should be no celebration in "almost" normality. Abnormal is abnormal and recognizing it as such will help you see the problem for what it is much faster.

Many loved ones have a hard time grasping the fact that a family member or friend is actually an alcoholic. Think about it, if you're wrong, there's no harm done, except for some hurt feelings. But if you're right, you have a chance to set up some boundaries so your alcoholic loved one has the opportunity to get better. Let's suppose you're not an expert on alcoholism. There are medical professionals who can determine if your loved one is an alcoholic. The trick might be getting your loved one there. If she suspects that she does indeed have a problem, she might fight you every step of the way when it comes to seeing a therapist or addictions specialist. There are many online tests you can take too. The following link will take you to an online test on the National Council for Alcoholism and Drug Dependence, Inc. (NCADD): https://www.ncadd.org/get-help/take-the-test/am-i-alcoholic-self-test.

Another package of denial comes with the alcoholic's behavior. Because so much happens when he's under the influence, his memory will be fuzzy or non-existent. Blackouts are when the alcoholic is awake and functioning normally by doing things such as driving, having conversations, or even working but the next day or the next week, he has absolutely no recollection of what happened. According to a longitudinal study by the National Institute on Alcohol Abuse and Alcoholism,

"If recreational drugs were tools, alcohol would be a sledgehammer. Few cognitive functions or behaviors escape the impact of alcohol, a fact that has long been recognized in the literature."[13] The study goes on to say that alcohol produces detectable memory impairments beginning after just one or two drinks. An alcoholic can experience *bloc blackouts*, where he doesn't remember anything for the entire period of intoxication or *fragmentary blackouts*, which are partial blocking of memory function for events that occurred while a person is intoxicated. These bouts of amnesia can make it impossible for him to recall any events, conversations, or experiences he had while under the influence of alcohol. Blackouts can last anywhere from 9 hours to 3 days. Therefore, you may have a conversation with your alcoholic loved one the next day, angry about something he said or did and he may have no recollection at all. Not only might he not remember, but also he may flat out deny that it ever happened. Hence perpetuates the insanity of the disease.

Denial & Disillusionment Stories from the Trenches

Recovering alcoholics tell stories about being in denial, some up until the very end. Many were in denial because they hated the word "alcoholism" because it conjured up mental images of a homeless person lining the streets and eating out of garbage cans. Others saw how bad their lives were but still didn't think it was alcoholism. And still some compared themselves to friends or family members who drank more than they did and justified their own behavior with a measuring stick uttering the phrase, "I'm not as bad as she is."

---

13 Aaron M. White PhD., "What Happened? Alcohol, Memory Blackouts and the Brain," National Institute on Alcohol Abuse and Alcoholism. http://pubs.niaaa.nih.gov/publications/arh27-2/186-196.htm

Tim

It was an emotional roller coaster. Sometimes I would wake up and say to myself, "You're a piece of shit. You've got to get your act together." And other times I would say, "I'm not that bad. Look at the homeless guy on the street." But in fact, at one point I became homeless in my alcoholism. Even when I became homeless, I said, "It's not the alcohol." It made no sense. It constantly lied to me.

I got so angry when people would tell me I was an alcoholic. I would reason with them. I would argue that I'm not an alcoholic because I got up this morning and did something besides having a drink. But in my early 30s, I didn't even argue because I knew I was an alcoholic. I wouldn't even go out of the house because I knew I was a hard core alcoholic.

Raul

From the very start, I knew how I drank and I knew how I used. It became daily for the last 4 years. And I held very strong to this notion, I only drank after 8 or 9 o'clock at night because that was my way of rationalizing that I didn't have a problem, granted I was smoking pot throughout the day. I wouldn't even go to a bar or restaurant with friends during the day because I knew how I drank. I drank for the effect and whatever it was going to take. And because of that, towards the end, I always tried to have enough.

Rachel

After two DUIs in DC, I moved to New York. I thought, *I'm not going to drive and I won't be breaking the law. I'll be O.K.* But that was a big lie. When I got so out of control and drunk, I would get into a cab and maybe not have money. Or if I had money I couldn't find or count it. A couple of times I remember cabbies yelling at me and telling me they were going to take me to the police. One time I gave the cab driver my iPhone just so he would let me out of the cab.

Cocaine came into my picture late in the game. I was a successful musician who believed that I was a functional alcoholic who just worked hard and played hard like anyone else in the entertainment industry and that I was entitled to this.

My value system in the course of alcoholism shifted. Your conscience becomes blurred. Behavior that couldn't have happened five years earlier happened easily.

Waldon

In a way I wanted to be an alcoholic but I didn't know what that was. I would lose jobs and I thought the employer or the supervisor was out to get me. I didn't know it was the alcohol. Every time I got fired, it was because they didn't like me. At this one department store, I was arriving late a lot because of the drinking. They didn't fire me but they transferred me to women's lingerie and I thought that was a punishment. I was mad and I quit. That was part of my denial.

Then I had two best friends who drank and we drank together but they went to college and they could handle it. We all drank alcoholically but they didn't have the disease. They finished college and got good jobs and I couldn't understand why I couldn't do the same things they could.

Dan

On the weekends I would wait until noon to drink because I said, "I don't want to be an alcoholic." So I would go out to mow the lawn and I'd hide a 6-pack of beer in the garage, put one beer on the lawnmower and keep going to places where my wife couldn't see, then change out the beer, so I could mow the lawn and have one beer but it was actually a 6-pack. I just wanted to be buzzed all the time but I couldn't do that or control it.

My dad once told me, "Don't drink hard liquor, you'll become an alcoholic." So I just drank beer and wine and convinced myself that I wasn't an alcoholic.

After we had our second child, we were having marriage problems, and my wife would complain about the drinking after I went to work events. I just thought she had a complaining problem. I got sent to an AA meeting from a marriage counselor. I went to the meeting wearing a suit and looked around and no one had a suit on, so I knew I didn't have a problem. But I sat down and listened to everyone. Some guy talked about taking a can of Pepsi, dumping it out and pouring beer in it. I said to myself, "See, I've never done that, so I don't have a problem." Two weeks later, I was doing the same thing because I thought it was a pretty good idea.

I had what they call, a high bottom, I didn't have any DUIs and I didn't lose anything materially. I did lose a job but not directly because of the alcohol. It was a sales job and I had the lowest sales that year. I told myself it wasn't because of the drinking but it was. I would go to my sales region, stay in the hotel, and drink. I never left the room to sell anything.

Lee

I didn't think I was an alcoholic because I had images of an alcoholic in my mind and I knew I wasn't that. I was making daily commitments not to drink but I could never follow through. I knew I was sick. I knew I was miserable. Suicide was becoming prevalent in my mind. I knew I couldn't live with alcohol, but also I knew I couldn't stop drinking. It did not seem to me that I had any options. It didn't occur to me to go to rehab. I just didn't think it was for me. I didn't think I was rehab material. I was by myself thinking this through. I was keeping a huge secret.

Action Steps to Bring to Light Denial & Disillusionment

Take one week at least and write down behaviors on a chart. I've used a spreadsheet for this exercise. You can use categories such as Accountability, Follows Through on Word, Tells the Truth, Abstains from Alcohol or Drugs, Comes Home, and Speaks Kindly. Then, for each day during the week, use the boxes to fill in "yes" or "no" for each one. You can also say a few words about each trait. For example, under "Follows Through on Word", if you asked your alcoholic loved one to pick up eggs and milk on the way home from work, did he follow through? Or under "Tells the Truth", if he lied, write, "no." After a week, you should be able to see patterns of alcoholic behavior that will help you come to terms with your loved one's illness.

CHAPTER 8
Lies & Deception

The art of pleasing is the art of deception.
—LUC DE CLAPIERS

Anyone who deals with an alcoholic or who is a recovering alcoholic will tell you that lies and deception are part and parcel of the illness. Honesty or lack thereof was a huge part of the conversation in my relationship with Johnny. I'm a big proponent of honesty (or at least I was) and have always trusted that people around me were honest too. Once the disease of alcoholism was unveiled to me, I noticed Johnny constantly lied about his drinking and once he started drinking he lied about most things. In fact, it became difficult to discern whether or not he was telling the truth about anything. I hated the way I became suspicious of him in all things. That wasn't me, trying to snoop around and verify information. Another thing that became a part of my disease was that I began to lie too. In the beginning I would pour out part of his drinks, or if he passed out I would dump the whole thing out. And when he awoke and asked me where his drink was, I would lie and tell him he drank it. Other times I lied out of fear. I knew he couldn't stand when I would tell his mother he had been drinking again. Yet, I felt I needed the support and for safety reasons (such as Johnny getting into a car to drive), I sometimes had to tell her. But when Johnny would ask if I had spoken to his mother, on occasion, I would lie and tell him I hadn't. The lies of addiction had gotten me too.

Many alcoholics are people pleasers but we as co-dependents or enablers are people pleasers too. Like the above quote proposes, people-pleasing is a form of deception or dishonesty. At first, you might disagree with me on this but instead of placing it in the category of honesty, let's put it in the category of authenticity.

Analyzing Why We Lie

Understanding why we lie is a great step toward dispelling the myth that we have to. Try to look inside yourself to see why you might deceive others at certain times.

1. Fear of Abandonment

Childhood trauma of a parent leaving through divorce, abandonment, or death can bring about current fears about abandonment. Children often blame themselves for a parent leaving so if you haven't worked out those feelings, you may carry them into adulthood. Many of us have fears of being alone so we lie to make sure the other person doesn't leave us.

2. Fear That I'm Not Good Enough

Strongly connected to the fear of abandonment, we all have fears that we are not enough. This fear may stem from infancy, childhood or adolescence. You may fear you're not pretty enough, thin enough, well educated or qualified enough. This particular fear comes disguised as low self-esteem. That's why people might lie on a resume or a dating profile.

When I was a kid, I was so ashamed that my parents were divorced, which was rare at the school I attended. As a consequence, I would constantly make up stories of having famous relatives to deflect away from the embarrassment that I wasn't like everyone else. In retrospect, it was sad. I felt I wasn't as good as the kids whose parents were married.

3. Self-Centeredness

We may lie to get our own way or to get ahead. This type of lying is generally more premeditated. For example, you might lie about a work colleague to make her look bad so you can get her position. Or it could be something as innocent as trying not to get in trouble, such as the popular kid phrase of, "I didn't do it. He did."

Adults do a fair amount of lying to get out of snafus too. Have you ever been pulled over by a police officer? "No officer, I was only going five miles over the speed limit."

4. To Manipulate Others

Closely related to self-centeredness, manipulation is a huge reason why many people lie. Alcoholic relationships are filled with manipulation on the part of the alcoholic and on the part of the co-dependent. Alcoholics manipulate to create the optimal environment for feeding the addiction. Loved ones manipulate to try to control or manage the drinking.

Lies of omission are a form of manipulation. For example, if your spouse wants to go out to happy hour after work but he knows you'll get upset if he tells you, he might go, come home late and then say something to the effect of, "Well, you never asked." Or "I didn't think it was a big deal, so I didn't tell you."

The reasons why these lies are destructive are because we use them to get someone to do something underhandedly or we take away the other person's freedom of choice to say "No."

5. To Avoid Conflict

Lying or deceiving to "keep the peace" is unfortunately a frequent behavior in an alcoholic home. It's also a red signal in any relationship, which indicates lack of trust and respect between parties. If I feel I must lie to avoid angering or upsetting you, there is not only mistrust and lack of respect for differing opinions, but also fear of one party holding more absolute authority or power over the other. Lying to avoid conflict is something that happens often in physically and emotionally abusive relationships.

6. Fear of Punishment

Similar to lying to avoid conflict, many people lie to simply avoid punishment. For example, take the two-year-old, who has been told not to touch the bag of cookies. She will lie, even with her face full of chocolate, to try and avoid her inevitable fate of being punished. The alcoholic will lie, telling you he's only had one or two drinks, to avoid being put out the front door or getting the car keys taken away.

Lies & Deception from the Trenches

Many recovering alcoholics have told me that alcoholism is entrenched in lies and deception. They have to lie to keep the machine of deception going in order to feed the addiction. Keep in perspective this is mental illness at its best. The disease tells the alcoholic she must lie and she begins to believe her own lies. At times, she's not even aware she's lying.

To add to the deception, an alcoholic will also have *delusions of grandeur*, telling you about the fantastic things they will do once they get sober or learn to control their drinking. They are thoroughly convinced they will "finish that law degree" or "become a famous Hollywood actor" and of course, you'll be sorry to be left in the dirt when they are rich and famous. Don't believe any of it. When your alcoholic loved one is able to get sober and save his own life, he will be an ordinary person like most people, regardless of what he tells you now.

Tim

I like to tell people, "Alcohol is such the liar." It's telling me all of this stuff that isn't true, like, "You're O.K. You don't need people. You don't need relationships. You don't need this job. You don't need this apartment." And I wouldn't have money to pay the bills because I could only spend it on alcohol, even when I had a lot of money. There was a time when I could make over $1,000 in cash as a bartender in some very high-end places. I could get off work at 10:30 p.m. and have $800 in my pocket and when I got home, I wouldn't have two pennies to rub together.

I lied to people about everything. When you're an alcoholic, people can tell you're an alcoholic. I would gulp down a bunch of alcohol in the first hour and then I could sit at the bar for ten hours. I'm the guy who would drink a 12-pack and do a few shots before going out with friends, just to be on the same level. I would lie constantly. I had many bars I would go to and all the bartenders knew me. I would go into each bar and only have one or two, to give off the persona of, "I'm the guy who doesn't drink a lot." But I would have one or two drinks at twenty bars.

Raul

I was at college and there was a point at which my parents had cut me off. My friends, the people I was associating with, didn't have any money, and I needed to drink. I would go downtown to the hotels and I would dress very nicely, I mean, I'm from an upper middle class family. I can speak well. I know how to interact well with people. And then, I would ask tourists for change just so I could get two 40s (Malt Liquor) so I could be "good" for the night and I'm thinking I'm a genius. I would ask for 55 cents to get on the bus. And the ironic thing was, I had no idea that I had a problem.

I used to be such a good liar. I went to acting school. I believed the lies. It kind of pisses me off how transparent I've become. I would meditate before I would lie to somebody's face. Oh my goodness, how much work it was to live that life. And now I can't even go to McDonald's and get a courtesy cup to fill it up with a soda.

Rachel

I was teaching dance classes and I would have a water bottle filled with white wine as I was teaching. All the times I wasn't passed out, alcohol was in the mix or about to be. Or I was so devastatingly hung over that I couldn't drink for one day or maybe two. I had to lie to others about my drinking, to employers and private clients.

Waldon

I had so many lies. I remember seeing this T-shirt in Georgetown that said, "I used up all my sick days, so I called in dead." That was me. I would use all kinds of excuses of people dying. I'll never forget this one. I called in on a Friday to tell work I had broken my leg. I couldn't come up with anything else because I had told them everything else. I was drunk at the time, but I had to think about how I was going to cure my leg by Monday.

I remember trying to make amends when I was in a program and I called the boss of that job and said, "You know, I had an alcohol problem back then when I was working for you." And she said, "We kind of figured that." I was in denial then too because I didn't know that they knew.

Dan

I was always hiding beer cans everywhere. My wife would always ask me, "How much have you had to drink?" I would lie say, "Oh, just a couple and I'm just really tired and I might have Lyme disease."

Lee

I lied about the amount I was drinking all the time. I deceived by hiding it. I lied to myself all the time. It's a lifestyle of lies and deception because it's trying to keep this thing going. I say it's like bobbing and weaving life. I would be falling asleep on the couch in between conference calls. So when your boss says, "What are you doing?" You don't say, "I was sleeping on the couch." I was bullshitting my way through every business call. I lied about where I was going and whom I was with to my son all the time.

When it came to the point that my alcoholism was really obvious, I was separated. So I didn't have to answer to anyone. I got away with it.

Action Steps to Live in Truth

When we have alcoholic relationships or even normal ones, it can be difficult sometimes to live in truth. Living in truth is about your own sense of integrity. It's living from a place of authenticity. The more you live in your truth, the more people respect you. It may not seem that way in the beginning but that's what it will become. Living in truth doesn't mean you need to hurt other people's feelings. You can be tactful, diplomatic, and compassionate.

1. **When expressing your truth, try to use "I" statements with feeling words.**
   For example, "I feel sad and afraid when you drink excessively."

2. **Admitting you don't know something is acceptable.**
   At times, you might think you need to have all the answers. If you're a female type, we seem to be plagued with thinking we have all the answers. If you are a co-dependent with the "Savior Syndrome", you might believe that you actually do have all the answers. My favorite answer these days is, "You know, that's a good question for Google."

3. **Answer, "Let me pray or meditate on that."**
   I will not take credit for this one. I heard Oprah Winfrey say this on one of her shows. I loved it immediately. From time to time, you might not be sure what your truth is. You might not even be aware of what your feelings are on a given topic. Instead of agreeing to do something you don't want to do or say something you don't want to say, just use that phrase. It buys you time to find your real answer.

4. **Go back and tell someone if you were untruthful.**
This is part of Step Five in the 12 steps of Alcoholics Anonymous and Al-Anon. If you're not comfortable doing this yet; at least think about it.

5. **Answer, "Not yet, but I'll share soon."**
Similar to "Let me pray or meditate on that." This answer says, "I know the answer. I'm just not ready to share it yet." It conveys the message that you need some space now. That is a perfectly acceptable answer.

6. **"No," is a complete sentence.**
I've mentioned this in a previous chapter and I'll emphasize it again. Many of us, myself included, feel we need to justify our decisions and answers. You do not need to justify an answer. When you make a choice, it's yours. And unless you care to make it anyone else's business, it's not.

As people in co-dependent or unhealthy relationships we've been used to feeling guilty for not giving everything to the other person or for not giving in to him or her. Your honesty, integrity, and self-worth are about you. Your "No" without explanation (unless completely warranted) will tell the other person, "I'm in charge of my decisions. I know what I want and what I don't and I'm ready to live with all and any consequences of my decisions." That is a display of maturity and self-esteem and will help you on the road to healthier relationships.

CHAPTER 9
Mental Mind Games That Drive You Crazy

*'Cause you're hot then you're cold, you're yes
then you're no, you're in then you're out, you're
up then you're down, you're wrong when it's
right, It's black then it's white, we fight, we
break up, we kiss, we make up...Stuck on a
roller coaster and I can't get off this ride.*
−KATY PERRY, HOT N COLD, 2008
CAPITOL MUSIC GROUP

Few diseases take you on a constant mental roller coaster like alcoholism and drug addiction. Each time I find myself on this wild ride, I'm reminded of the Katy Perry song *Hot N Cold*. The guilt, shame, and blame game, the Dr. Jekyll and Mr. Hyde personality and a low sense of self-worth make up the parts of this crazy moving machine.

Ready for a Crisis

While most of us in normal day to day living have a healthy dose of denial about tragic life events and our own mortality, children of alcoholics or those having lived long term with an alcoholic are always in impending crisis mode. They are either cleaning up from a mental (and sometimes physical mess) or bracing themselves for the next one. In fact, for children of alcoholics, crisis mode becomes the norm. When things are calm, they feel agitated and uneasy. Many children of alcoholics grow up to be emergency room doctors or nurses or part of the military or police force since they tend to do well in times of crisis.

By living with an alcoholic, you learn to be alert and ready to react. One step-dad told me he even slept with his pants on at night just in case his alcoholic and drug addict stepson did something bad.

Lack of Consistency

Unpredictability is the first factor in the roller coaster ride of alcoholism. You never know what you're going to get, who you're going to get and when. Will it be Dr. Jekyll or Mr. Hyde this time? It seems like you're always waiting for the other shoe to drop. You are constantly in Fight-Flight mode. You're walking on eggshells and it doesn't feel like you can ever relax.

One day, the alcoholic is extremely loving, kind, compassionate, giving, and normal. The next day she's angry, deceptive, distant, and drunk. Or the good days could go on for several days in a row and you're led to believe that all is well. Then, "Bam!" out of the clear blue, it hits again and you're left reeling. You're wondering what happened and how it happened.

Your foundation is completely unsteady. You start to feel unsure and insecure in your relationship. You don't know where you stand. The seeds of lowered self-esteem begin to take root. Your mind plays tricks on you. You can see that sometimes your loved one is nice and loving and you feel she loves you. But the next day, she acts like she hates you. What is going on?

Shame, Blame, and Guilt

As you will read in the testimonies below, the alcoholic's sense of shame and guilt are enormous. He doesn't comprehend what is happening to him, why he does what he does and how to get out of it. He wakes up in the morning wondering what happened the night before and the guilt and shame keeps piling up from the last time.

Now enter you, his loved one. You come into the picture confused, angry, and upset, because he has yet again done terrible things while drunk. So you yell, scream, or sulk and as a result he blames you for some things or all things. All he is doing is spilling his own guilt out on you because he can't deal with it.

As a result you feel ashamed for yelling and blaming him because inside your heart, you know it was the alcohol and that he probably doesn't remember half the stuff he did or said anyway. And so, continues the ride of blame, shame, and guilt.

Getting off the Damn Roller Coaster

You have a choice not to ride this roller coaster anymore. You know the old adage, "It takes two to tango"? If you step off, he'll have to ride it by himself. It takes a long time to master this skill, but it's doable.

You are not doing it to hurt or get back at him, but only to save yourself. Take note, he will be angry that you're no longer joining in on the ride. He may even throw a temper tantrum. That's okay, it's his stuff and he needs to face it to start getting better.

Here's how you can get off the crazy ride:

- Don't react to his behavior.
- Walk away when he gets critical, rude, or starts to blame.
- Don't ask him about his drinking behavior such as, "How many drinks have you had?" Or "Did you stop at the bar on the way home?"

- Make alternate plans when he bails out on plans you both had together.
- Make other friends who are healthy and sane.
- Don't talk about him negatively to friends, family or anyone who knows him.
- Don't take what he says personally.
- Don't check up on him to see what he's doing.
- Stay silent with a smile because silence can be golden.

By getting off the roller coaster, you are giving his stuff back to him to deal with. You've been his seat belt and safety net and when you step out of the way, you can let him feel the consequences more quickly.

A Dual Personality: Dr. Jekyll & Mr. Hyde from the Trenches

Most alcoholics are in such hardcore denial that they can't see the differences in their personalities. One thing they are aware of, sometimes, is that they manipulate people to believe different things about them. Alcoholics learn to be master manipulators to get what they want in order to feed the addiction.

Tim

There were a lot of personalities and they were trained to what environment I would be in. There was a more sinister, not feeling personality. When I was drinking I could do things I would never think of doing. My relationships were based on what people could give me.

When I was sober, I would have a more compassionate side to me to where I would truly care for some people. But as soon as I started drinking it became, "What can I get out of this situation?" And people knew that. That was the drunk, sinister side.

Waldon

I tried to hide how bad it was in relationships. I would tell some people that I didn't drink at all. But I always looked for people who drank. In most of my relationships I was trying to be this "other person". It got to the point where the alcohol took over. It kept me unemployed

You always had a fantasy that you weren't where you were and that the situation you were in wasn't real. Especially when you are drinking, you had the best ideas. I would say, "I know what I'm going to do. I'm going to go to school and become a doctor." I had all of these ideas and then as you're going along, you're drunk and you lose your job and you have no way of getting into school.

I dropped out after my second year of college because the professor wanted us to form groups to do a project and meet after school. I knew how I drank and I didn't think I would fit in. I knew how my lifestyle was. I needed to be around people who drank and smoked marijuana.

Lee

I blended in because a lot of women in this area drink a ton of wine. I also pre-gamed and post-gamed. So people didn't see me drink very much. I would go out, have a few drinks, and then drink at home. I hid it from my husband at the time. When I started drinking again in 2006, it came back very quickly. I thought I was going to break the habit and just drink like a normal person and I just never did. I still didn't think I was an alcoholic.

Guilt, Shame, Blame, and Self-Worth from the Trenches

Imagine pouring water into a glass and when it's full, you keep pouring. Water flows out of the glass, onto the counter, over the counter and onto the floor. The guilt and shame an alcoholic feels on a daily basis is like that overflowing glass. In the book *Power Versus Force*, author Dr. David Hawkins explains that shame and guilt are two of the lowest human emotions we could possibly experience. Hawkins goes on to say that shame is the equivalent of conscious suicide and guilt, its neighbor, pulls down the whole level of personality. People who live constantly with both shame and guilt are prone to suicidal tendencies, psychosis, psychosomatic disease, accidents and a whole host of other negative emotions.

Tim

For a long time, that guilt and shame made me want to drink to oblivion. "I'm not living up to my potential in life. I know I'm better than this, but all I can do is drink and spend all of my money on drinking and live in these horrible studio apartments. You know Tim, you're never going to meet a girl with all these empty bottles everywhere." But it made my hand heavier. I realized my life was horrible. So why not drink?

I would always blame others. It started with my mom and how she was living her life. If it was my brother, I would say, "You drink just as much as I do." It would boil my blood and make me so angry when a bartender would say, "You know you're an alcoholic." I would think, *You're the biggest jerk in the world.* I would say, "I'm not an alcoholic. I'm the guy who's paying your bill right now. If I wasn't here, you wouldn't make any money." I got so angry when people would tell me I was an alcoholic.

Raul

I put my parents through hell. My dad could see it clearly but my mom was in real denial. I would play on that. And that would cause a rift between them. But I'm accumulating this deep down, this guilt and shame that I'm never trying to take a look at. No wonder I don't like myself. No wonder I'm not good enough. I have mountains of shame, guilt, and demoralization that I'm never going to deal with. And that's what the program (AA) has taught me.

Waldon

I still felt like a victim. I felt the reason I'm doing this is because it's everybody else's fault. The blaming is easy. I didn't feel guilt. But maybe I felt shame from losing stuff and getting fired. After a paycheck, the next day I wouldn't have any money because I would spend it on drugs and alcohol when my co-workers, who had money, would be going to lunch together the day after payday. If I didn't spend all of my money, I would be too hung-over to come in. I felt ashamed for that.

Dan

I remember reading my daughter a bedtime story and she wouldn't go to sleep. I would get so mad because I wanted that open beer bottle that was downstairs just waiting for me. I would get mad and would later feel guilt and shame and I hated myself. The solution to the heaviness of the guilt and shame was to pour more alcohol to get rid of it and it was a bad cycle.

I would blame my wife for my drinking. I would go to meetings and say, "My wife is why I drink." They would say, "Did she ever get you in a headlock and pour alcohol down your throat?" And I said, "No." Then they would say, "So she never made you drink." And I would answer, "Well, she made me thirsty." It was always something, but it was never me. It was my boss or my wife. If only they would treat me better. What I found out later was that it was my self-centeredness. I am the problem.

Lee

The shame was the constant. It was waking up every day and saying, "Oh my God. What did I do? And who was there? Who saw?" I did things that were not super ladylike when I was drinking. I made out with guys at the local bar or hooked up with them. I'd flirt with people's husbands. I'd cheat on my own boyfriends.

Action Steps to Clear the Mental Mind Games

1. Take ownership for what you've done.
You can't own others' faults, actions, words, or deeds. But you can own up to what you've done. Try not to feel guilty or ashamed about it. Make amends when possible.

2. Look inside of your own self-worth and discover the truth about your sensitive areas.
Here's an example: When your alcoholic loved one is drinking, he calls you a "fat cow" and you call him "a drunken ass". Inside, it hurts that he calls you a "fat cow". (By the way, calling him "a drunken ass" isn't nice either.) Look inside yourself. Do you feel that way about you? If so, what can you do to change it? No matter what he says, it should not change your self-esteem or self-worth.

Johnny used to say, "old lady" to me when he was drunk. I used to get so mad. Then, I had to look inside. Did I feel old? My answer was, "No." Did I think I looked old? Again I came up with, "No." Then, why did it bother me? I came up with the answer that the only reason why it bothered me was because it just represented words of disrespect. I then, shared with him when he was not drinking that I didn't like it when he said those words to me.

If you can check in with how you feel about you, hurtful words will have less power over you.

3. Don't argue or debate.
No other thing will keep you on the crazy roller coaster like arguing and debating. Your alcoholic loved one loves this because it gives her

an opportunity to keep you on the ride, blame you, and turn the argument around to make you look like the bad person. Remember she is a master of deflection. She will always deflect the energy away from her and put it onto you. As hard as it is, silence is the only thing that will keep you off the ride.

4. Look for the good in your alcoholic and tell her.

I can imagine that you're ready to call me some choice names right now so let me speak your words out loud. "What? You mean to tell me after she calls me names, mistreats me, lies, manipulates, and blames me for everything, I'm now supposed to compliment her?"

Yes. She is always feeling low, down in the gutter low. She feels worthless, unwanted, and depressed. Her self-esteem is lying somewhere around her toes. Any air of self-confidence she exudes is an act. She needs you to notice her good points. She needs you to lift her up in any authentic way you can, then maybe she too will be ready to get of the roller coaster.

Part Three
Inside The Soul

*I am a soul. I know well that what I shall render
up to the grave is not myself. That which is myself
will go elsewhere. Earth, thou art not my abyss!*

-VICTOR HUGO

While matters of the heart and mind are tangible, real, familiar, and feel as if you could hold them in your hand, soul matters feel more evasive.

Addiction is the constant search for something more to this life. It is a desire to make union with the Divine. Addicts are reaching for the blissful joy of Source. Momentarily, they do attain it. The euphoria they experience gives them great pleasure in peak state moments. But these moments are artificially induced which leave a deficit, lack, and greater emptiness than ever before. That is why they seek stronger and more intense feelings through the object of addiction. There is never enough. For nothing, other than the real experience of spiritual soul connection, can give the seeker solace.

The glimmer of light, in the depths of darkness and despair, comes from an awareness the alcoholic has to reach toward it. If he is to stay rooted in his body and mind, he will surely die. For it is access to the soul that makes him start to come alive once again.

CHAPTER 10
The Search for God

*We need to find God, and he cannot be found in noise
and restlessness. God is the friend of silence. See how
nature - trees, flowers, grass- grows in silence; see
the stars, the moon and the sun, how they move in
silence... We need silence to be able to touch souls.*

- MOTHER TERESA

Since alcoholism touches every single aspect of a person's life, finding a spiritual connection to a Higher Power is essential in recovery. I have not yet met an alcoholic in long-term full recovery who does not embrace a Higher Power. The entire basis for 12-Step groups revolves around the development of one's spiritual life.

People of all religious backgrounds, spiritual penchants or no sense of religion or spirituality have been able to work the 12-Steps successfully. Many of the recovering alcoholics I interviewed had no concept of a Higher Power prior to sobriety. Yet, every single one of them found their own concept of a Higher Power in the course of recovery.

The metaphysical component of recovery cannot be denied. Alcoholism takes everything away from you. It wrecks your physical body, relationships, mental health, sense of dignity and strength, and your sense of self. One alcoholic explained it to me as a "soul sucking" disease. At the end, as you hit rock bottom, you are completely empty inside. There is something supernatural that takes place when an alcoholic reaches the point where he's searching for something higher than himself.

The Search for God from the Trenches

Have you ever reached the point where you felt abandoned and all alone? It may have been a time when you lost someone to a break up or death. Maybe you had no money and needed to pay the bills. Or perhaps it was a time when you just felt lost. Did you ever reach out to God? Or ask if there was a God?

> *Lost and insecure, you found me, you found*
> *me, Lyin' on the floor, surrounded, surrounded*
> *Why'd you have to wait? Where were you? Where*
> *were you? Just a little late, you found me.*
> *– THE FRAY, YOU FOUND ME, 2009*

Rachel

My mom had a spiritual leaning because she wanted to become a nun before she had me. She worked hard to send me to Catholic school. There was God. I had a really positive experience. Then, my mom shifted to another church, Unity. Even though I would go to church, I would leave church and go to brunch with friends and I didn't know what was going to happen. I felt like a hypocrite. I used to try and use spirituality to address my disease but it was still too big for me.

Now I go to the Lutheran Church because I work here. There's an expression that goes, "God brought me to the program and the program brought me back to God."

Waldon

My mother belonged to a holiness church. They are the type who speak in tongues, run around and pass out. I felt so bad because I didn't fall down when the pastor touched my head. I didn't feel anything and I was the only one.

At first when I went to AA, I thought they were going to teach me how to drink, where it didn't affect my life so badly. I thought I would be able to control it or stop for a while and start again. Then, I got that they were telling people to stop. I figured, they might have something because I kept hearing people talk about tools. I would think, *What tools are they talking about and where do I get them?* Then, they started to talk about God. In my mind, I instantly went to my mother's church. And I said, "This is not going to work because it didn't work for me then. He never guided me. I didn't get it." I was crying that first day. It hit me that that's what they were talking about and I was so depressed. I actually cried. I felt like meetings were going to be my hope. But I didn't see how it could work.

Dan

The first year in the program, I couldn't grasp a Higher Power. I said, "That's good for other people but I'm going to use the rooms, the other people as my Higher Power." And it worked for me.

I dabbled in it. I tried to go to church and I had a lot of fear. God was a scary thing for me. I figured the way I was living my life, I was going to be burning in hell anyways so I didn't want to have anything to do with it. So based on that, I just kept my distance.

Somewhere in the midst of working steps four through nine I thought, *Yes, maybe there is a Higher Power. I don't know what it is. But I'm going to start turning stuff over and see what happens.* And little by little the more I did that, things would happen and I would start to feel this peace about myself. I would see people around me and changes getting made in them. I would say, "That is a freakin' miracle."

So things were happening and I started taking notice. First of all, my head wasn't filled with alcohol so I was more clear-minded. I could see things as they were happening. I could feel changes in myself. And the more I let go, the more peace and serenity I found. By the time I was done with step twelve, I had had a spiritual awakening. Upon exploration, I could see, hear, think and feel miracles happening in my life. I never had the "burning bush" or a flash of light and I still haven't. But I still have these awakenings.

Lee

I was raised Catholic. I have always been a spiritual seeker. But I had gotten away from the Catholic Church. I tried a lot of different spiritual paths; Taoism, Buddhism, I was every -ism. I was always trying to figure out what my concept of God was. I remember writing it out because I wanted to be able to tell somebody if they asked me. Even in the midst of alcoholism, my knowledge of faith was what kept me alive. It was the knowing that everything was happening exactly as it's sup-posed to and everything is going to be okay.

My real concept of God didn't develop before doing the steps because that's what the steps help us do. Doing the steps clears out the debris so we can have an open space for the God of our understanding to step in and do His work. It did help me because I was open to the steps and how they worked.

I don't think anyone comes into AA with a real connection to a Higher Power because if we had it, we wouldn't be where we are. I think I had an intellectual concept, but not in my heart.

Action Steps to Help You Search for Your Higher Power

1. What notion of God or Higher Power did you grow up with?
2. How has that changed today?
3. Do you ever remember a time when you felt completely at peace?
4. Do you believe there is something bigger than yourself at work in the universe?
5. How can you separate spirituality from religion?

CHAPTER 11

Surrender

Let go, and let God.

Most of us who have co-dependent and enabling tendencies have what I call the "Savior complex". We are under the belief that we have to swoop in and save the day. One thing I struggle with each and every day when it comes to my alcoholic is, *I am not powerful enough to save him on my own*. But part of my disease says *I am powerful enough. If I don't save him, who will?* The real answer is, "God will." And that has always been the case.

I especially struggle with surrender in my alcoholic relationship because in my particular spiritual belief, I am to be a steward of God's love. I am commissioned by God to help those in need. I am to help those who are vulnerable, lost, and sick. And I *know* he is sick, lost, and in desperate need of help. But I need to embrace the fact that it's not up to me alone, it's up to God as to when and how he gets help.

When God created us, He gave us free will. We have free will choices in everything, even in seeking a relationship with Him. If I have free will choice, so then, does my alcoholic loved one.

The maddening part in all of this is that I know he is not free. He is shackled to his addiction. His judgment is cloudy, murky, and abnormal. The alcohol doesn't allow him to think clearly enough to get out of his own insanity.

Yet, even so, he has to at some point and that point is called hitting rock bottom. Rock bottom is when the alcoholic has some sort of epiphany, realization, or awakening that he needs to change. Sometimes the rock bottom comes from heavy alcohol withdrawal symptoms. At times it comes when she loses everything or winds up in jail. For each alcoholic living in sobriety, there came a time when he or she hit that all time low and it is vastly different for each one.

My rock bottom, as someone who loves an alcoholic, came when I truly realized that there was nothing I could do to make him stop. It's funny, when you struggle against God for so long, fighting him, wrestling for the right to decide someone else's destiny, it drains you, because God always wins in the end. It reminds me of the story of Jacob, in the book of Genesis in the Bible, who literally wrestled with God, in the form of an Angel, all night long. God let Jacob win but he broke Jacob's hip to show him humility. When we struggle against our Higher Power instead of surrendering, we may seemingly win for a time, but we are left with injuries and scars. And that is our disease.

For an alcoholic, the point of rock bottom is usually the starting point of sobriety. It's where the alcoholic finally realizes he can't continue to drink, he can't do it alone, and he needs help from his Higher Power if he is to continue to live. And that epiphany is called surrender. It is the basis for the first three of the Twelve Steps of Alcoholics Anonymous and it's when the alcoholic realizes he is powerless over alcohol and that he needs his Higher Power to help restore him to sanity.

Hitting Rock Bottom from the Trenches

Every alcoholic's bottom is different. Some alcoholics must lose everyone and everything before they realize they need help. Others realize it before they lose a lot, which is referred to as a "high bottom". In most cases, he must absolutely hit this himself.

Tim

I had a grand mal seizure. People die from grand mal seizures. I was sitting in my apartment and drinking about three-fifths a day[14]. I had stopped eating. I would just drink, pass out then drink and pass out. I was hallucinating and hearing voices. This night I was sitting with an eight-inch chef's knife, from my kitchen, in my bed with me. I was drinking a bottle of vodka. I was staring at my veins. I couldn't get comfortable. My body had hot flashes and cold flashes. I had a seizure and it put me on my knees. That night was a strange night for me. I started speaking in tongues, which had never happened before. I was so scared because I thought I saw the devil in my room or a demon of some kind. Then I just started praying. I just started saying every prayer I could remember. I lived across the street from a Catholic church. They had a statue of a saint. It was three o'clock in the morning and I remember I went across the street and got on my knees and started praying in front of the statue. And I said, "If there is anything out there to help me, help me!" That was my last night of alcohol. My brain was so befuddled. I tried to remember the Lord's Prayer and I couldn't remember it all. Whatever I could remember, I said it over and over. I laughed and cried. I was having an emotional breakdown. The next morning I finally woke up and I poured out a half bottle of vodka and I said, "That's it. I'm never touching alcohol again." There was a lady I used to

---

14 One-fifth of alcohol is about the equivalent of one-fifth of a gallon.

work with who got sober so I called her up. She came over and said, "You need to go get a bottle of vodka and taper off for three days because you can really hurt yourself." When she left I didn't do it. I shook it off for three days and detoxed. And I had seizure after seizure.

After three days, I called my mom and told her I needed to go to the hospital. And for the first time in a long time, she jumped and was there immediately. A week before I had called my mom and asked her if she could take me to church because I felt I needed something in my life. But somehow she didn't come or something. So she brought me to her house and we were waiting for my stepfather to come home so they could both take me to the hospital. I was sitting outside in her backyard talking to trees because I was still delusional. Yet, I had the clarity to ask her why she hadn't picked me up for church the week before. She told me the story that she had tried. She knocked on the door for ten or fifteen minutes and had a key so she let herself in. She came into my bedroom and I was on the floor and she thought I was dead. And she said, "You weren't really breathing. And so I put a mirror under your nose. Then I could see that you were breathing. So I just left." She told me, "I really was hoping you were dead. Because after 33 years...I couldn't do it anymore Tim. I can't watch you die. You're dying in a little apartment. You have no job and no friends. And you know, I just can't do it anymore."

Raul

I got my first DUI and was put on probation. I couldn't pass the urine test so eventually my probation officer said, "I'm sending you to jail." So I did three months in DC jail. One week before I was to be released, I had to go to jail in Pennsylvania for five extra months for an altercation I had gotten into five years before (for which I was still on probation). But it was amazing, because during that last month in DC, I was on the phone with my girlfriend saying, "Get the pills ready and make sure you have my alcohol." It was funny because I was ready to start ripping and rolling again after those three months. But my Higher Power had a different plan. Thank God I had those extra five months. Because when I got out, I wanted to drink. I wanted to say, "Good job Raul, you made it. You deserve it." But I had a flash that said it's going to get worse and you're going to come right back here. So I went to an outpatient place and they kept telling me to go to AA and get a sponsor and I got sick of hearing it, so I went. Even then I never thought I was an alcoholic. Alcoholics were weak people. I had no idea.

Rachel

I had been fired from one of the jobs that I loved the most. I was constantly late, constantly forgetting and so unfocused. It was chaos.

I was in crisis. By the end, I got kicked out of my apartment. My housemate found me in the kitchen with friends doing lines of cocaine. Then I had to move in with a friend with whom I used to drink. And he and his boyfriend got so scared of my drinking that they hid all the alcohol and locked it away. The doors were shutting. My mother who lives in Virginia said, 'You can't stay here. I can't take it." She told me, "You don't have a job. I'll take your cat and you need to get into one of these programs." So I told her if she came to take me, I would go. She was so excited and so I went.

I thought going to AA would work because I had worked the 12 Steps before. But I was doing gigs in bars, clubs and restaurants and the people in AA told me, "You know it's going to be hard for you to get sober while you're still doing that." I didn't want to hear that because I had worked so hard to get to that place in my job. I had put my career before my life. It had to come to me saying, "I don't care if I ever perform again live. I don't care if I see any of these people again."

Lee

For me 2011 was a yearlong bottom.

I couldn't go on living like that. The bulk of it was hangover and sickness. I kept thinking if I could just think up a cure for the common hangover, I might still be drinking today. I did everything I could do to push through the day every day and the only thing that could make me feel better was alcohol.

I was dating a guy that year and we had broken up like four times. He was probably an alcoholic too. It was a very toxic situation. I was a wreck by the end of that year. And he was watching this. At first no one was paying attention to me and then he was paying attention through all of this. My son was starting to notice too and was very unhappy with me. I was starting to embarrass him. He was making nasty comments to me about stuff. Right around my birthday, in October, I planned to take a 30-day break from alcohol, in January. And I set it that far in advance, on purpose, just to get everyone to leave me alone. I did it because I started to sense that the wheels were coming off and people were noticing. I was more worried about the people than I was about myself. January 1st 2012 was the day I was supposed to quit and everybody knew it and so I had to do it or else that was going to be a problem.

I went cold turkey on January 1st. About four days into it, I was talking to the guy I was dating and said, "When this 30 days is up, I'm only going to drink when we're out to dinner or a special occasion or something." I was already planning my drinking. He sat me down. I think that was the only reason this man was ever in my life, was for this one conversation. He grabbed me by the shoulders, looked me in my face and said, "Can I just point out to you some things I've observed over the past year." He pointed out time and time again of things that I had done. It was the first time that anyone had ever confronted me head on because I was always able to explain things or nobody would see it.

`I started crying. It was my first surrender moment. I cried. He was kind. He didn't yell at me or make me feel bad about myself. He said, "I think you need AA." I said, "You're right." I picked up the phone and called a friend of mine and she met me on January 7th at my first AA meeting and I've been all in ever since. I haven't picked up a drink or Xanax since January 1, 2012. I didn't touch anything.

Surrender from the Trenches

Surrender truly is all about letting go and letting God take over. It is the space of realizing, "I'm not in control. God is." It's liberating and freeing. You feel as if a giant weight has been lifted off your shoulders.

Tim

I remember in The Big Book there's a paragraph that says something like this (I'm paraphrasing), "God is never elusive. He never shuts the door on anyone. He allows anybody in. And it doesn't matter what your concept of God is as long as you have one." In the beginning I had childish notions and was in a very child-like state when it came to my Higher Power.

I was working with this older guy who was 40 years sober. Everybody called him the Yoda of AA. And he told me, "I know you're a big guy. And I can see you haven't prayed much in your life. But you're going to have to get on your knees and you're going to have to repent. And you're going to have to find a way to talk to God. The way I want you to do it is every morning on your knees." And every morning that's how we would start, on our knees and we would do the first three steps and I would say, "God I am powerless over alcohol. Please give me the strength to stay sober today. God please direct my will and my life today." Every day during the first year of sobriety, I would do that. And at the end of the day, I would get down on my knees again and say, "God, thank you for today. I know it was you."

Rachel

I had six months sober on March 20th and it was a wild whim, where I drank. I was still in my program. After being six months sober, I still entertained the notion that I could drink responsibly and that's not how it went down. It was full of mayhem. I went to my therapy appointment at 6 p.m. after drinking since about 3 p.m. My therapist pointed out that I was under the influence and I fell apart. I said, "If I keep relapsing like this I want to die." She said, "I can't let you leave now that you've said that. I'm going to call your program, your mother or your sponsor. So she called my sponsor who came to get me. And then my sponsor brought me to the emergency room and stayed with me. Then she called my program. I was so thankful that my program gave me a second chance. They do not give you a third. I got back at 11 p.m. And the very next day I went back to zero in the program. I had to give them my phone and do all of this all over again. That week was Holy Week and

Pastor Karen who had a good connection over at my program said that all who wanted to come to services could come. And I knew I had to go. I don't know why but I just went. I got communion and went to my seat. There was no pew to kneel on so I kneeled on the floor. I got on my knees and just cried. And the prayer was different. I swore if God got me sober that I would stick with this faith path, because I've always been a wanderer. I was just crying out to God, Jesus, the Holy Spirit, the Saints, and to my grandmother to save me. I made a deal with God and that was a turning point. I came everyday thereafter and did the same thing. It was just grace.

Waldon

I had gone to AA since 1978 and would go periods without drinking but I could never get that one-year.

Seven years ago I was homeless again. At that time, I was 49-years-old and I just couldn't deal with it. I wound up in a psych ward in a hospital. By that time I had AIDS. I remember them telling me I had to take this medicine so I started running around my bed to exercise, in the hospital, and I think that gave me hope. My plan was to check out and commit suicide. I ended up going back to a support group for people with HIV. Then I started going to an AA meeting downtown. I was still on the fence about this "God" thing. But this time around I didn't try to go back to school, I didn't worry about a job or career. I said, "I'm just going to try and do this thing I've been trying to do for 30 years." I said, "I'm going to test out this God thing." I had read all of the literature and I got a service position at meetings. I went to meetings every day and just showed up and seven years later, it still works. I gave in. And I had to find my own way of believing. I did it based on things that happened.

Dan

I had gone to seven meetings in seven days and I hadn't had a drink in seven days. That's the longest period I had gone without drinking. Then my wife went on a business trip, at the end of those seven days, and the kids were probably yelling and screaming and I said, "You know, it's not worth it. Screw it!" So I went out and drank again. The next day I came to a meeting. There was one guy who was always asking me, every time he saw me he said, "How are you doing?" I told him, "Not good." And then I said, "My wife went out of town and I don't know what happened. I drank last night." He said, "Did you tell her?" And I said, "Well, I didn't get caught so why would I tell her?" And the funny thing is she didn't even know I was trying to stop drinking. He said to me the words I needed to hear and never forgot, "Well, if you don't get honest, you can't get better." I had to get honest with myself first and say, "I really have a problem and I'm totally powerless. And I really need to get help." For some reason that hit me right between the eyes like a two by four. So I went home and told my wife. I said, "I'm trying not to drink. I've been going to AA meetings. I went seven days sober and you went out of town and I drank. I can't drink because I'm an alcoholic. I can't drink safely." At that moment, I felt a big weight lifted off my shoulders. It was that surrender of "I'm done. I've got to come clean." My life was not unmanageable at the time but it was unbearable. I was sick and tired of being sick and tired. I wasn't living at all. It was just pure torture.

Do Family Interventions Work to Help an Alcoholic Hit Rock Bottom?

An intervention is where family members, friends, and perhaps a professional counselor or therapist come together to confront the alcoholic about his drinking. Typically, the alcoholic is unaware that the intervention will take place and he's usually surprised, by arriving for a different event or appointment, to find a circle of friends ready to intervene. The end goal of an intervention is to get the alcoholic to realize that he has a disease, that he needs help and to get him into a treatment program immediately.

Loved ones of the alcoholic will take turns reading letters to him explaining the behavior they've seen over time. The counselor or medical professional will then explain the course of action he needs to take to stop the progression of the disease. In the best case scenario, the alcoholic will be emotionally moved, let his guard down and agree to enter treatment.

We did try an intervention with Johnny at one point. While he sat and listened to each person, he ultimately did not let his guard down, nor did he admit that he had a problem or agree to treatment. However, the good thing about the intervention was that it got the conversation started. It helped lift his alcoholism out of the darkness.

Interventions can and do work. Statistics show that interventions are about 80% successful in getting your loved one into treatment. But you need to have leverage. For some, they have the boss, at work, who says the alcoholic can't return to work until he's sober. Spouses have given ultimatums during interventions if the alcoholic doesn't agree to treatment. Children are good leverage too. The sober spouse can write up an agreement that all visitations must be supervised (provided that the sober spouse moves out or asks the other to leave) until the alcoholic spouse gets help.

Interventions can help raise the bottom. A great book to help you with an organized intervention is, *Love First: A Family's Guide to Intervention* by Jeff and Debra Jay.

Action Steps to Improve Surrender Into Your Life

1. Realize and repeat the first step of Alcoholics Anonymous that you are powerless over alcohol and that your life has become unmanageable.
2. Relinquish control of your situation over to your Higher Power. Realize that you are not in control over another person's drinking and that you never were. Remember the 3 C's: You did not cause your loved one to drink, you cannot control his or her drinking and you cannot cure his or her alcoholism.
3. Make a list of things you can actively change in your life and a list of things you cannot change.

CHAPTER 12
Who I am sober?

"Don't pick up a drink or drug, one day at a time. It sounds so simple. It actually is simple but it isn't easy: it requires incredible support and fastidious structuring."
— RUSSELL BRAND IN *THE GUARDIAN*,
SUNDAY, MARCH 9, 2013

n the midst of a relationship with a drinking alcoholic, it can be difficult to imagine that she can be any different. When we're caught up in this mindset, we're still thinking that alcoholism is a personality defect rather than a physical, mental, emotional, and spiritual disease. The truth is that people do get and stay well. They can return to a normal way of thinking and being. However, often their personalities look much different in sobriety than they ever looked like when they were still drinking. Moments of sobriety, in the midst of addiction, do not reflect what a person will look like in total sobriety. Remember that alcohol addiction is all encompassing and when a drinking alcoholic has sober moments, he's still focusing on how to get the next drink. His brain has been severely altered by the alcohol and it takes from several months up to several years before his brain heals and his thinking is restored to more normal patterns. As a result, most recovering alcoholics have little idea of who they really are in sobriety. This realization can create a lot of anxiety in your alcoholic loved one. Imagine waking up one day and not knowing who you are. That is one of the reasons that early sobriety can be extremely challenging and also one reason why many alcoholics relapse.

Early sobriety comes with confusion, anger, and frustration. You may find your alcoholic loved one to be irritable and at times unbearable when he's trying to get sober. Think about it from his perspective. He is losing his best friend, his confidant, and his only coping mechanism for handling emotions. In sobriety, he's now faced with the issues, problems, and consequences for all of the actions he performed during addiction. Overwhelmed doesn't even begin to describe what your alcoholic loved one is going through in early sobriety. That's why attending rehab, Alcoholics Anonymous on a daily basis, and getting a sponsor are all important in staying sober.

Early Sobriety from the Trenches

For a non-alcoholic or "normie" as they affectionately say in Alcoholics Anonymous, it can be difficult to understand what your loved one is going through in early sobriety. Imagine being dropped in the middle of the desert with no water. You might feel panic, rage, anxiety, fear, and be completely lost. You fear your life is ending and you only have a few days to live.

Tim

The first month sober I had no clue. I was just shell shocked. It was really hard being sober and looking at my life. And that is what they asked me to do. I was still in a horrible apartment, by myself, writing down things about my life and saying, "I'm the worst person I've ever met." And I've said this before.

I would kill a man for the things that I've done to myself. If somebody else did this to me, they would be dead. I would go to prison and it would be over.

In the beginning I wouldn't say, "God or Higher Power" and I wouldn't get down on my knees when the guy told me to get down on my knees. I kept thinking, *This is stupid.* But then I started looking back and realized that everything I had prayed for had come true and to this day, it keeps happening.

Rachel

I worry about people I used to hang out with. I have a great friend in New York who is a partier. And I worry about communicating with her, not about alcohol or anything, just about cats or something. I worry because it's a trigger.

Dan

I hit a moment of surrender in my drinking. I was totally done. I couldn't do it anymore. I couldn't go on living like that. I give up, white flag. That was a hell of a blow to my ego. My ego was like, "You can do this. Come on, let's go for another round." The first part was easy, but going through the rest of the steps and doing my moral inventory, going through my personal defects, my fears, resentments, and harm I'd done to others was more difficult. I wrote it down on paper and I said, "I'm filled with ego, false pride, and self-centered fear. That is the basic undercurrent of my life. I'm going to lose what I have or I'm not going to get what I want." And I had driven my life on that. I was trying to control everyone and everything and it was through being nice, being mean, through tricks, through deceiving, and it didn't work. My life was crap. I couldn't live like that so I had to drink.

I got to an emotional bottom. When you get into long-term sobriety and you don't have alcohol anymore, you need to find something else. If not, you're going to change back. So, it's an ongoing thing. About a year ago, I was up for another job and I started getting into that obsessive thinking where I was trying to control everything and I came very close to taking a drink. But then I came to surrender again. I came to this place where I could just let go and say, "You know what, I'm not in charge. That was an actor trying to be a director in this world." I'm not the center of the universe; God is the center of the universe. And all I have to do is play my part and play it the best I can. At that point, the weight of the world came off my shoulders. That's what I was trying to look for when I drank, that peace and serenity. I could never find it. I could never take that big, deep breath. It's a new freedom I never had before.

Lee

I don't remember much of the first couple of months of sobriety except that I knew I had found a home. I knew I was where I needed to be. I started feeling better. It was the biggest blessing ever.

Deciphering Confusing Information on Getting Sober

There is a lot of conflicting and confusing information out there about getting sober. Some of that information may come from books, videos, or news reports. Your alcoholic loved one might try to convince you that he has created the perfect program to get sober. In his speech, he may even be extremely convincing. Let's partition off information so, as a loved one, you're able to see clearly and also perhaps make a decision for yourself as to what you wish to believe.

Yoga, meditation, hypnosis, going to the gym, self-help books or herbal medicine will help someone get sober, are the claims some people purport. While all of these things are helpful in creating a lifestyle change and also in supporting someone, as he or she is getting sober, they will not make a person sober. Almost every single person I interviewed admitted that, at times during the worst episodes of drinking, they would make plans to wake up the next morning and jog, eat organic food, go play tennis or do yoga so they could stop drinking. And every single person failed 100% of the time. Johnny made promises to start a fail-proof gym routine that would get him sober, at least a dozen times over the course of three years and never went past day two. If your alcoholic loved one is telling you she has the perfect sobriety program, that she has invented, please don't buy into it. Would you trust your garbage collector to fly a commercial airliner for you? The answer is, "Of course not." Your garbage collector has no firsthand knowledge on flying a commercial airliner (unless that was his former job). In other words, what does your alcoholic loved one know about sobriety? The answer is, "Absolutely nothing." So she can't have the perfect solution on getting sober.

Alcoholism is a physical, mental, behavioral, and spiritual disease. The chemistry of the physical illness is omnipresent in an alcoholic's body. The mental aspect is overbearing if not addressed. And the lack of complete faith in a Higher Power to get him through the day without drinking will cause him to fail every single time.

Healthy practices are part and parcel of a complete sobriety program but they are not the program itself. The issue with a multi-faceted disease is that every level of the disease must be addressed if the person is to get well.

The genius in a 12-Step program is that it addresses all of the issues in this multi-faceted disease. When an alcoholic follows the program at 100%, he is successful. Twelve step programs have also withstood the test of time. Alcoholics Anonymous has been around since 1935 and has helped millions of alcoholics get and stay sober. Most in-patient and outpatient rehab programs integrate 12-Step programs into their overall program because they know it works.

Managed Drinking

There is a philosophy out there on managed or controlled drinking. An alcoholic who has crossed the line between heavy drinking and alcoholism can never successfully drink, ever again. Remember, alcoholism is a chronic, progressive and fatal disease, the two key words here being: chronic and progressive. Chronic means it is ongoing, it never goes away. And progressive means that over time it gets worse. If the alcoholic continues to drink alcohol under any capacity, the progressive nature of the disease will make him worse (more obsessive, increasing doses of alcohol and having increased withdrawal symptoms) and eventually lead to death.

A heavy drinker, who has not crossed the line into alcoholism, can successfully manage drinking.

"I'll Just Stop Drinking Then."

When an alcoholic stops drinking, he is a "dry drunk". His physical body will eventually return to normal functioning. His liver and kidneys will heal and other parts of his body will no longer suffer from the toxins from alcohol abuse. However, abstaining from alcohol, for an alcoholic, does not make him sober. He will get sober only when he heals the other parts that made him ill in the first place. All the personal character defects will still be there. The wounds from the past will still plague him. The lack of faith and surrender will cause him to remain ill under other capacities.

Crossover or Switched Addiction

Many alcoholics have multiple addictions such as a drug or tobacco addiction. As alcoholism intensifies and progresses, some alcoholics seek a greater high or deeper intensity and turn to various drugs to magnify the effect. Other alcoholics grow into the addiction with drugs alongside the alcohol. If your alcoholic loved one agrees to stop drinking alcohol and get sober, look out for crossover addictions.

While it's also harmful to your loved one's health, smoking (tobacco) is a frequent crossover addiction in early sobriety. However, tobacco will not interfere directly with substance abuse sobriety so you shouldn't worry too much in the initial stages. Red flags would include switching to drugs such as cocaine, marijuana, heroin, crack, or crystal methadone. Prescription drugs such as Xanax, Ativan, Adderall, Ritalin, or any prescription medication classified as a narcotic or controlled substance are in the dangerous or red flag category for recovering alcoholics and should be avoided. Because crossover addiction is prevalent for recovering alcoholics, it's important that your loved one is honest with his healthcare provider that he is in recovery for alcoholism as ask for medications, when needed, that are non-addictive.

In rehab programs and 12-Step groups, your alcoholic loved one in early recovery will learn about switched addiction and what to look for. Besides drugs and tobacco, switched addiction can equate to compulsive gambling, shopping, eating, sex, or even fitness.

Action Steps in Handling Your Loved One's Early Sobriety

1. Hands off.

You've been waiting for this day for years or decades. Your alcoholic loved one finally admits she needs help. With your take charge attitude and co-dependent tendencies (I say that with the greatest amount of affection), you whip out your spreadsheet of the best rehabs, inpatient and outpatient centers, your list of AA meetings and list of sponsors for your loved one. How do I know this? Because I've been there.

Your loved one, unless she's a minor child, needs to choose her own method of treatment and her dedication to the program. It's acceptable to initially recommend detox in a hospital setting and drive her there. At detox, they will tell her what to do to get and stay sober. If she's going to AA, they will tell her everything she needs to know to work the program.

In other words, you cannot possibly hold her hand 24/7 and watch every move to make sure she's not drinking.

2. Relapses are normal.

I didn't know this and I didn't believe it. A little over half of the recovering alcoholics I interviewed had relapses in the beginning. So you've got about a 60/40 shot that your loved one will relapse. It's not the end of the world if it happens as long as he gets back in the program. Have you ever met someone who's tried to stop smoking? I'm sure you've heard them go back at least three to four times before stopping completely.

It can be frustrating but remember this is not your journey; it's his.

3. Your alcoholic loved one is not used to experiencing emotions without alcohol.

Life can be scary, surprising, unexpected, frustrating, and joyful all in the span of one hour. Now magnify that times twenty-four hours a day. Most alcoholics have had alcohol as the only coping mechanism for 10, 20, 30 or 40 years. Now delete that security blanket and insert life.

Anger is a common emotion in early recovery since most alcoholics don't understand what's happening to them emotionally. After the first week of detox, your alcoholic loved one may experience Post Acute Withdrawal Syndrome (PAWS).[15] Some of the symptoms of PAWS include emotional outbursts or lack of emotion, anxiety, difficulty dealing with stress, difficulty sleeping (having vivid dreams or nightmares), memory problems, trouble thinking clearly, and dizziness. Depending on how long your loved one was drinking, the symptoms can last anywhere from a few weeks to several months.

4. Be patient and do not lose hope.

After waiting for so long, it can be difficult to have to wait some more. It's important for you, now more than ever, to be patient with your alcoholic loved one.

---

15 "Post Acute Withdrawal Syndrome (PAWS)," UW Health, Health Facts for You, 2015, University of Wisconsin Hospitals and Clinics Authority, http://www. uwhealth.org/healthfacts/psychiatry/7228.pdf#toolbar=1&statusbar=1&messages= 1&navpanes=1

CHAPTER 13

God's Miracles

Out of difficulties grow miracles.

—JEAN DE LA BRUYERE

A breakthrough to surrender in addiction is nothing less than miraculous. Ego, pride, and self-preservation must all be stripped away in order to create space for the Divine to enter. When this happens, there is but a small window where the light can enter before the ego rushes in to slam it shut. In that small space, we can experience moments of perfection.

Miracles from the Trenches

When you experience a miracle, it completely changes your perspective. What you didn't think was possible all of the sudden becomes real. It widens the realm of possibilities. The sphere of possibilities doesn't change; you change.

Tim

My mom and stepdad took me to the hospital. I remember the ride. I was still losing it. But the sun was going down on the way into Baltimore and all of the sudden I saw this flash of the light. It was a plane taking off into the sun and it did this flash. But something rushed over me, like a sense of calmness. The calmness said, "Hey, you might get through this." Then all of the sudden my brain started working again.

I was sitting in the emergency room in downtown Baltimore. I checked myself in. We all sat down and the place was packed. It all of the sudden occurred to me that I was making the hugest mistake of my life. I felt, *If I don't get out of this now. I could die.* And that is what the voices were telling me too. I was trying to convince my parents to leave, so as soon as they left, I could go to the bar. And I knew where there was a bar right around the corner. But my mom said, "No, it's O.K. we'll just stay here another minute or two." And the next thing you know, a nurse comes out and calls my name. I knew it was God. He was telling me I had had enough. It was amazing. The hospital staff said, "We are really scared. We think you're going to die. You are on the verge of a heart attack. You're heart rate is so high." They shot me up with Valium and I woke up upstairs and did eight days of detox.

After detox, the same lady who had helped me came and took me to AA. I don't remember anything profound about that meeting. But what I do remember is something inside me had changed. Something changed after I prayed that prayer during the grand mal seizure that night. It was an honest prayer. My prayer, that night, went something like this, "God, I know I'm not one of your favorites, but could you just kill me so this will stop? If you can't kill me, help me." I knew when I was sitting in that room, he was helping me. He was changing my life and I just had to listen.

Raul

When I got broken up with eight months ago, this relationship had provided me with a lesson. It represented so many things because I just wanted to understand what happened and I didn't get that. I didn't get closure. Where is my trust in my Higher Power that I need that? How can I live in that trust?

In the midst of that break up, I went on a walk and I was in a lot of pain where I thought about drinking. And then I got mad at myself and said, "Raul, of course you're going to think that, you're an alcoholic." There were tears of pain and anger. I was on the floor with raw emotion. And my tears of sorrow and pain turned to joy in the depths of it because God was there. I was saying, "God, do you see this? You see what's happening? Do you see this? Because I don't think you want me to be like this..." And God said, "Yeah, I do. You're exactly where you're supposed to be." That's when my tears turned to joy. All of a sudden this entity that used to be out there, is now in here. (Points to his heart) I felt that. I liked it so much that I searched for it everywhere. But you know it's not going to happen like that.

I celebrated at Dupont Circle and a bunch of us went out to dinner. I was taking a shower and my eyes started tearing up because I'm a part of something. I have friends who love me. And then the feeling started to fleet away and I was like, "Wait, no, I want it back." I wanted to go back into that moment. As part of my addiction, I always want more.

Waldon

I was going to this meeting on this Friday. I heard there was an anniversary on the other part of town and I was running late. I thought, *I'm going to let God make this decision. If the bus comes, I'll get on it and I'll make this meeting.* If not, I'll go to the other meeting. The bus didn't come so I ended going to the meeting near me. As it turns out, I had the wrong day. It wasn't the anniversary that night. So that must have been God working. I thought, *Maybe that's how I'm going to get it, if it happens through circumstances.* Things happen for a reason. That was my entryway into belief.

I don't have that strong belief like others. As the literature says, "It's better to believe that there is a God and find out that there is, then to not believe and when you die you find out that there is and then it's too late."

Dan

When I was all in, I was all in. I knew sobriety had to take front and center stage. It was scary but then it wasn't as long as I stayed close to the program. I had people all around me. And I had a sponsor I talked to every single day. They call it the "pink cloud". I was like "Wow! This is incredible." I remember waking up for a nine o'clock meeting on a Saturday and I was like, "Oh my God. It's so bright and beautiful. And the colors…" I couldn't remember the last time I woke up that early and left the house. It was like the Wizard of Oz movie. Before I didn't notice things while I was drinking. I used to drive out in my truck with the windows rolled up and the music blasting because I'm trying to drown out the noises in my head, the guilt, shame, and fear. So I was driving to my meeting with my windows down in the spring and I hear the peepers, these little frogs, and I thought, "Wow! I remember those when I was a kid. I wonder where they've been." They had been there all along. I had never noticed them. I didn't have that connection. Just stuff like that. It was so moving for me. I started to experience life again.

Action Steps to Create the Miraculous in Your Life

Miracles start with an open mind. It's realizing you don't have control of this great big universe. It's also realizing there is something bigger than what you see, hear, think, and feel. Your sphere is much grander than you could ever know. You can start creating that space for miracles to occur in your life.

1. Get silent.

Silence is the only space where you hear God's voice.

2. Spend time in nature.

Experience the miraculous all around you.

3. Observe with the eyes of a child.

Look for things you normally wouldn't see. Look up as you get out of the car. Divert your attention to a painting in your favorite coffee place. Watch the bugs at work on the ground.

4. Let wonder and awe overcome you.

Aren't you in awe by the way your computer or cell phone works? I am, at different moments every day. Find the miracles in the ordinary. I see these little caterpillars crossing the sidewalk and wonder how they manage to stay alive. There are so many things surrounding you at all times which are no less than miraculous.

CHAPTER 14

Compassion, Understanding & Love for The Alcoholic in Your Life

God's dream is that you and I and all of us will realize that we are family, that we are made for togetherness, goodness and for compassion.
— DESMOND TUTU

Relationships come in all shapes and sizes. Perspective is a big part of being in a relationship with an alcoholic. As people who love alcoholics, we can have a tendency to over-exaggerate the flaws in an alcoholic and fanaticize about erasing those flaws. Can you relate to this fantasy? "If only he would stop drinking or using and get well, our relationship would be great." I have had this fantasy so often.

Human flaws don't just come disguised as alcoholism. People can be anxious, mean, angry, violent, depressed, distant, emotionally abusive, and more without being alcoholics or addicts. I know you know this intellectually, but since you are in a relationship with an alcoholic, it can be easy to forget this fact.

I know husbands or wives who place career before family and the spouse, left at home, feels neglected. I've heard of people with anger issues who are no more than social drinkers. In relationships, many people lack proper communication skills to be able to develop intimacy and vulnerability between parties. In other words, don't let yourself get downtrodden thinking that everyone else has it good, and because your loved one is an alcoholic, your life sucks.

Here is the upside. Recovering alcoholics, who are working a program, do more in the way of human development than most humans living without addiction. The 12-Step process truly digs deep into the core of a person and when she works it in earnest, she accesses the best qualities of relationship and being human. So while the magic wand you've been wishing for all these years doesn't work in an instant, have your hope lie in the fact that in recovery, your alcoholic loved one will be better off than perhaps your neighbor, friend or other family members.

Guess what else? When you work the 12-Steps too, imagine what kind of explosive good your relationship will have when you both are living at a different level. You will go from being dysfunctional, unhealthy and destructive to being, healthy, inspirational, and giving with enormous boosts to your self-esteem.

Have Patience

I can't emphasize enough that true sobriety and recovery take time. Nothing can replace the gift of time. Since alcoholism is a brain disease, it can take up to three years for the brain to heal completely. The human body is an amazing miraculous machine. His brain will grow new neural pathways in sobriety and the shrinkage caused by the alcohol will be replaced by new cell growth. His liver and kidneys will become restored and go back to normal functioning. He will start to sleep better without the need for drugs or alcohol. He will become a regular contributor to life and the responsibilities held within. Relationships will be recreated. And his life will take on new meaning.

Recovery is possible and this is the final leg in the painful part of the journey so try and stay the course.

The Biggest Change Now That They're Sober

In my interviews, I asked recovering alcoholics how they saw themselves after those initial stages of sobriety and how they see themselves now.

Tim

Everything I've prayed for in my life started happening. And it keeps happening and happening. It's amazing!

I was three months sober and really fearful that I was going to have to go and work in a bar again because that's about all I knew how to do. Then a guy in AA said, "Well, what do you want to do?" I said, "I want a job at the cable company or I want to work at a bank because they are 9 to 5 and they don't have alcohol there." And the reason I wanted a job at the cable company was to get free cable. The guy laughed and suggested I go pray about it. I thought, *That's the dumbest thing in the world. Why would he tell me to go pray about working in a bank or at the cable company?* But I did. I went home every night and prayed about it. I got called for an interview at a bank for a part-time teller position. I had a two-hour interview with the lady at the bank. She loved me but said I would be a terrible teller but that there was an opening for a full-time sales position. I got that job. In two years I was the top sales person and it was all because I was learning to show up, be on time and be clear-headed. My humor was starting to come back and I was starting to feel like a real person again. I was starting to work with other guys and helping them get on the path to sobriety. I wanted to pass on that knowledge that life isn't over.

I demanded God to prove to me that He was real. And He did. Now my heart and my faith are in Him completely. My whole life is for Him. My perception has changed drastically from the first day of sobriety.

Raul

My life is very full. I now have the ability to let go more and more and trust. I'm able to show up, I'm able to be a part of, and I'm able to face being uncomfortable without drugs and alcohol.

Rachel

Recovery is so much more. If people think that you can just stop drinking, that's not the case. The -ism is still there. I have to do a lot of self-care to stay ahead of it. I was putting my career ahead of my life and it cannot get out of balance like that again. It's about respecting my needs as a human being. I have to sleep eight hours. I see a therapist. I see a psychiatrist. Nutrition is important to me. I always have to be on the lookout for that weird compulsive behavior.

Waldon

I feel good feeling good. I don't feel good feeling bad anymore. That is the biggest change. When I felt bad, I would talk about it. I remember when I first started going to treatment, and when I shared, I always shared something depressing. I wanted people to feel sorry for me. Now I share about running fifteen marathons.

I had a back injury and I've been in misery for the last several months. It's worse for me now because I don't feel good feeling bad. So this has been hard.

I feel good having a life. There was a time when I couldn't hold twenty dollars for twenty minutes. Now, I just bought an expensive elliptical machine for $2,600. I don't have that kind of money but I have credit now.

My life has changed a lot.

Lee

Everything has changed. When I came in I was vice president of a company and I used to do podium presenting. I had to drink and take Xanax to speak in public. Now I speak in public for a living. I lost that job on the day of my last drink because we lost our funding. God works in crazy ways. That job did not need to be my job in recovery because of too much travel and too much alcohol.

I'm just a completely different person with honesty. I don't have shame and guilt anymore. I'm a mom and a great example of sobriety for my son who may or may not have a problem. I show up. I remember everything. I do what I say I'm going to do. My career that I lost twenty years ago, I got back. I can have a relationship that's normal now. I sponsor women. I do volunteer work all the time. God stepped in and completely restored me to who he created me to be. All the crap that I was wasn't me. So it's not that I've changed, it's that all of that crap is gone. I don't have to lie about anything. I'm authentic.

The Past Life Remains in the Past

Relapse can be a scary thing for a recovering alcoholic. All recovering alcoholics must develop skills and ways to cope with life. It's not as easy as turning off a switch. The wisdom that comes from long-term sobriety is deep and worth sharing.

Tim

The disease is elusive and evasive. During my first two years in sobriety I went to nine funerals. And these were people who were working on their sobriety. Some of these funerals I went to were single car crashes with no skid marks, overdoses, and people I had just talked to the day before.

AA was the only place I went for a long time in sobriety. I cut off all ties with everyone else in my life. At about my six-year mark in sobriety, I stopped going to AA and my Bible and my church became my program. I still have friends from AA and keep close ties with them.

I don't have fears from my past. I don't struggle at all when it comes to tendencies toward drinking now. I look at drinking as just a horrible thing. Sometimes I get overcritical but I keep my mouth shut when people at work say, "Hey, we're going to a bar." I almost want to give them the lecture, "Hey, it is killing you." But they aren't alcoholics so I don't need to do that. There might be one in the mix, but in my mind, I'm like, "Oh, it's so horrible."

Raul

What this program has done for me, what AA has done for me, being an alcoholic, is to give me an avenue to take away myself, and to get in touch with my soul. I always knew something else was there, always. I just kept getting in my own way. Drugs for a while gave me that connection but this does it too. I think the steps are in order for a reason, because I need to address this stuff.

Waldon

I feel confident. But I don't want to get overly confident. I still have the disease. I haven't had the urge to go back there because I like how I'm living now. It's easier to stay sober than to get sober.

I call it floodgates. Once you open the floodgates, it is so hard to close them again. I experienced it too many times. Now, once they're closed, it's like it has a little lock. You just put it in there and keep it closed. And if you try to mess it up or mess with it, it's gone. I know that from experience.

I made sure I didn't make running my new addiction. I read everything on running. I would purposely take off one day of running so it wasn't an addiction. God maybe gave me a message with my back being injured where I couldn't do any running at all. I had to take off a few months.

Dan

Things are going to happen that I'm not O.K. with and that's life. But now I have a way to get through it. I have faith that I will be taken care of. It's night and day from hating the world and if there is a God, I hate him too. I'm all by myself, the loneliness. Now, I'm never alone because I do have a relationship with my Higher Power. And even if things aren't going my way I still have a loving, caring Higher Power that's just like a father figure. The unconditional love that is there is something I've never felt with any person. But I can try to pass on that unconditional love that I'm getting to another human being and that's where the gifts are.

A Message from the Alcoholic to Loved Ones

Trapped, lonely, and desperate, are all feelings each alcoholic felt before recovery. I asked each person what they would have wanted to say to their loved ones in the midst of addiction and what advice they would give to those whose loved ones are still drinking.

Tim's Message

I think the loud and clear message is, "I'm dying here." And they could see that. But I couldn't tell them. Emotionally I had no level of saying, "It's killing me and I need help." I wouldn't say it. I would say I needed help with bills and money. But what I really needed was to be removed from my life because I was dying.

My advice to others would be, "You need to stop all enabling." And if I could have given my mother advice back in the day, I would have told her to stop enabling. Because she would give me money and help me out of the jams instead of saying, "This is it. Stop drinking or you're done." That's the advice I give people now. If a person is truly an alcoholic, they're not going to hear the same things you hear. You have two choices (as a loved one), either stay in that lifestyle or leave. And the only way he's going to stop is if it hits him, himself.

Raul's Message

About a year and a half into sobriety, I started hanging around with this girl who was deep in addiction to alcohol. I know I shouldn't have, but I did. I tried to live vicariously through her. But it came to a point where I was on the phone with her and I couldn't convince her of anything. She was so caught up in her addiction. I imagined how my parents must have felt. I couldn't do anything. She had to want it for herself. At that point I was just enabling and I had to let go. If my mom could have let go a little sooner, I probably would have hit my bottom a lot sooner.

Waldon's Message

It's not that I don't love you and that I'm trying to be like this or that I want to be like this. I have a problem. No amount of love or whatever you show me, if I'm in the midst of that, you can't get me out of it. The addiction is just too strong.

You have to be patient but you also have to be firm. You can't enable. You need to find balance between being a complete enabler and totally cutting them off.

You can't argue with them and say, "You'd better get into treatment." Or "You've got to do this or that." Arguing is not going to do it. They're going to blame you. You do have to give them ultimatums.

It's a tricky balance because some people will die if the conditions become too harsh. If you say, "You have to go, you can't live here." They might go out there and die. I was in a program once, a sober living house, where you sign an agreement that if you drink or even if you are suspected of drinking, they can put you out even after you pay your rent or security deposit. That happened to me where one of the guys said, "We suspect you of drinking and we voted you out." It was a hundred degrees outside, I had been sober for eight months but I relapsed. So as a consequence I lost my apartment and my job and I was suicidal. In situations like that, it might help to take him to a detox, or the psych ward at the hospital.

A Message From the Author to Loved Ones

My mission is to help lift the shroud that covers the disease of alcoholism and you can help. Did you know that currently, 90% of all actively drinking alcoholics are not receiving help? I believe part of the reason is that there is still an enormous social stigma surrounding the disease. Together we can shatter the stigma. How? The answer is one person at a time.

I was recently at a TEDx conference where I heard, Michael Botticelli, Director of the White House National Drug Control Policy, talk about his confirmation hearing for his position. Mr. Botticelli is a recovering alcoholic and drug addict, who is 29 years in recovery. He's also a homosexual man. He explained that during his confirmation hearing, the fact that he was homosexual was not mentioned once. However, the fact that he was a recovering addict almost prevented him from getting the position. At one time, people who were gay, lesbian, or transgender might be barred from certain positions or areas of social status. Now things are more open to greater equality.

A disease like alcoholism is just that, a disease. No one chooses the disease of alcoholism. Granted, it is a disease, which affects a person mentally and socially. But would you be embarrassed to say a loved one is suffering from anxiety or depression?

It's time we start talking about alcoholism as a disease in social circles. You can educate people about the disease. You can stand proud, strong and give bullet points when someone asks. Your tone of voice and body language will either send the message of acceptance or of shame. I'm asking you to help me transmit the message of acceptance.

I hope this book has given you strength, power, and hope. The diagnosis of alcoholism doesn't have to be a death sentence. It doesn't have to be the end of your relationship either. If you do your part, God will do His. There are few diseases where the loved one can have a direct impact on the outcome of the disease. Your strength and resolve in letting your alcoholic fall is that impact. Your unconditional love and firmly set boundaries are the medicine he needs to find sobriety. My hope for you is that the transference from survival to a thriving, satisfying relationship and life comes quickly for you. I pray you will become a beacon of light for others to follow. I'm sending you my love and the collective love from all the people who have come before you in your situation. You can make it and so can your alcoholic loved one.

Q & A: QUICK ANSWERS TO YOUR
DOUBTS ABOUT ALCOHOLISM

Below is a quick guide on common questions about living with an alcoholic loved one. Feel free to email me questions at michellefondinauthor@gmail.com. I will also be answering questions I receive on my YouTube channel: https://www.youtube.com/user/mfondin

Q: Shouldn't my loved one's doctor be able to detect his alcoholism?
A: Most family or primary care physicians are not properly trained on identifying the classic symptoms of alcoholism. A 1998 study published by the National Center on Addiction and Substance Abuse at Columbia University found that only 1 percent of primary care physicians identified alcoholism when presented with classic symptoms of alcohol addiction in an older woman.[16] Since alcoholism still wears a shroud of shame, many doctors fear embarrassing their patients if they ask too many questions surrounding their drinking habits.

Q: Isn't a little alcohol good for you?
A: The studies that show that a small glass of red wine daily can enhance cardiovascular health don't necessarily look at other lifestyle habits such as eating a diet with increased vegetables and fruit or eating olive oil instead of saturated fats and exercise. The benefits you can receive from one 4 oz. glass of red wine can also be found in red or purple grape juice.[17]

---

16 Jeff Jay and Debra Jay, *Love First: A Family's Guide to Intervention*, (Center City, MN: Hazeldon, 2008), page 76.

17 Katherine Zeratsky, R.D, L.D., "Does grape juice offer the same health benefits as red wine?", Mayo Clinic Healthy Lifestyle and Healthy Eating, http://www.mayoclinic.org/healthy-lifestyle/nutrition-and-healthy-eating/expert-answers/food-and-nutrition/faq-20058529.

Alcohol is the most damaging drug to the human body. It affects all organs and is the cause of many diseases. A study by The George Washington University Medical Center in 2003 showed that 25% of all patients admitted to our nation's hospitals and 33% of all emergency room patients have alcoholism or are problem drinkers. However, most of these patients were not seeking help for alcoholism but rather were treated for alcohol-related illness and injury.[18]

Q: Do I need to quit drinking alcohol just because my loved one is an alcoholic?
A: That is entirely your decision to make. If you find, however, that after reading this book, you might have a problem with alcohol abuse or alcoholism, I would highly recommend you get into a program even if your loved one is not yet on board. If you are a moderate or social drinker and choose to continue to drink alcohol, that shouldn't affect your relationship positively or negatively while your loved one is still drinking. However, once your loved one gets sober and is in recovery, you may want to reevaluate. Early sobriety is extremely challenging for an alcoholic. If he lives with you, the home needs to be alcohol and drug free until he's more stable in his recovery, which can take up to two years. In the event that your alcoholic loved one doesn't live with you, try to make family events alcohol-free until your recovering loved one feels strong enough to resist the temptation.

Q: Wouldn't throwing away the alcohol save her?
A: Oh, don't I wish that were true. It can be tempting to throw away bottles of alcohol when your loved one isn't around. But, and I say this

---

18 *Ensuring Solutions to Alcohol Problems Primer 3.* The George Washington University Medical Center, April 2003.

with the greatest amount of compassion, it won't work. It will only backfire on you. The compulsion to drink for an alcoholic is so strong that she will do anything she can to get more alcohol. If you throw away her supply, she will not only be angry with you but she may even blame you for making her drink more. Remember, she needs to reap her own consequences for her actions so that she comes to the realization that the drinking is out of control. I once read a statement that hit home. It said, "If you throw away her drink, that may have been the very drink that would have put her over the edge and caused her to get help."

Q: In some books I've read about "detachment". What does this mean and isn't it cruel?
A: The principle of detachment is close to that of surrender. What you're detaching from is the drama of the alcoholism. You're detaching from the pain, suffering and manipulation of being in a relationship with an alcoholic. You are also detaching yourself from her problems. You're allowing the space for your alcoholic loved one to feel the consequences of her actions while taking care of yourself.

Q: I'm still not sold that alcoholism is a disease. Isn't it just a question of willpower?
A: When my alcoholic loved one used to say he didn't have a disease, I used to come back with, "Well, if it's not, you're just an awful person?" There is solid, scientific evidence that alcoholism is a disease. The basic definition of a disease is that it must have a harmful effect on the body, mind or both, and has signs and symptoms that clinicians can use to differentiate one disease from another. Alcoholism includes a progressive loss of control over alcohol use, a preoccupation with acquiring alcohol, a continued use in

spite of adverse consequences, and a pattern of relapse to alcohol consumption.[19]

Q: Can't my husband and I just work through couples' therapy?

A: Many therapists won't work with couples if one person is an actively drinking alcoholic or drug addict. The reason is because of the deceptive nature of the disease. Your husband is probably in the state of denial. He also lies all the time to everyone and to himself. Real work in therapy comes from a place of honesty, openness and vulnerability. If he's not ready to get real with himself, no amount of therapy will help your relationship.

However, don't despair. Once your husband is ready to get help for his drinking and abstain from alcohol and any other mind-altering substance, marriage counseling can help. He may need several months of a combination of rehab and AA before he can mentally manage to work on his marriage but when he's thinking more clearly, it's a great way to improve things on the home front.

Q: My wife admits she has a problem and says she'll change. How do I know if she's serious this time?

A: It's very difficult to know if an alcoholic loved one is serious about seeking help. What I can tell you from my experience and the experience of countless others is that your wife needs to initiate help herself. You can suggest some things, such as, "I've read that most alcoholics need a medically supervised detox before starting AA or a rehab program. When you're ready I can drive you to the hospital." You can also direct her to the Alcoholic Anonymous website. Other than that, keep your hands off her recovery.

---

19 James W. West M.D., *The Betty Ford Center: Book of Answers*. (New York: Pocket Books, 1997), page 29.

You will know if she's serious by her actions. If she is making her recovery a priority by going to detox, rehab or meetings, and you see adequate changes, then you'll know she's serious. At AA meetings, she'll be encouraged to do 90 in 90, which means 90 meetings in 90 days and to get a sponsor. Also, because of red tape in hospitals, when she does decide to go to detox, take her to the emergency room. Hospitals admit alcoholics much faster through the emergency room than through evaluations and assessments, which might take much longer to schedule. You can call your local hospital ahead to see if they have an addiction detox program and if they don't, go to another one that does.

Q: I'm afraid if I kick my adult alcoholic son out of the house, I'll never see him again.

A: Your fears are valid and understandable. As parents it can be difficult seeing your child suffer through addiction. Your entire job as a parent was to keep your son safe, make sure he was fed, clothed and had adequate shelter. Now that he's an adult, he's making his own choices, including the choice to feed the addiction. While you now know he has a disease, he still needs to feel the consequences of his choices like all adults. Remember when he was learning to walk? You had to let him fall several times before he could feel stable on his feet. He needs to fall and feel the bumps, bruises and find his own stability. As for not seeing him again, it may happen but it's unlikely. Alcoholics may be infuriated at family members who see the truth but those people will be the first ones he seeks when he's ready to get help. And he will be the most thankful to you for letting him fall on his own.

If you are worried that he may harm himself or if he has threatened suicide, you can call 911 or call the National Suicide Prevention Lifeline 1-800-273-8255. You can also tell him, "Son, we love you and when you're ready to seek the help you need for your alcoholism, please call us and we'll get you to a hospital."

GLOSSARY OF TERMS

Adult Child of an Alcoholic (ACOA)- The term "adult child" is used to describe adults who grew up in alcoholic or dysfunctional homes and who exhibit identifiable traits that reveal past abuse or neglect.

The Big Book- The main book used by participants of Alcoholics Anonymous published by Alcoholics Anonymous World Service.

Blackouts (Alcoholic)- Periods of memory loss for the events of any part of a drinking episode without loss of consciousness.

Codependent- A dysfunctional type of relationship where one person enables another person's addiction or mental health problems. The relationship is one-sided, where one person does most of the giving, and often results in an emotionally or physically abusive relationship.

Delirium tremens (DTs) – The most severe form of alcohol withdrawal in alcoholics and includes tremors, hallucinations, anxiety and disorientation.

Delusions of Grandeur- The fixed false belief that one possesses superior qualities such as fame, omnipotence, genius or great wealth. Alcohol and drug use can intensify these episodes.

Dual Diagnosis- A co-occurrence of alcoholism and another psychiatric disorder.

Enabler- A person who encourages or enables negative or self-destructive behavior in another.

Grand mal seizure- Loss of consciousness and violent muscle contractions. This type of seizure is the most frequent.

Post Acute Withdrawal Syndrome (PAWS)- A host of symptoms caused by prolonged alcohol withdrawal and maybe the leading cause of relapse among alcoholics in early recovery.

Wet brain- The common term for a condition called Wernicke-Korsakoff syndrome. It's a type of dementia caused by end stage alcoholism. It is caused by a deficiency of vitamin B1 (thiamine).

The Rooms- Informal term, used by recovering alcoholics, to refer to Alcoholic Anonymous meetings.

The Twelve Steps of Alcoholics Anonymous

1. We admitted we were powerless over alcohol—that our lives had become unmanageable.
2. Came to believe that a Power greater than ourselves could restore us to sanity.
3. Made a decision to turn our will and our lives over to the care of God, as we understood Him.
4. Made a searching and fearless moral inventory of ourselves.
5. Admitted to God, to ourselves, and to another human being the exact nature of our wrongs.
6. Were entirely ready to have God remove all these defects of character.
7. Humbly asked Him to remove our shortcomings.
8. Made a list of all persons we had harmed, and became willing to make amends to them all.
9. Made direct amends to such people wherever possible, except when to do so would injure them or others.
10. Continued to take personal inventory and when we were wrong promptly admitted it.
11. Sought through prayer and meditation to improve our conscious contact with God as we understood Him, praying only for knowledge of His will for us and the power to carry that out.
12. Having had a spiritual awakening as the result of these steps, we tried to carry this message to alcoholics, and to practice these principles in all our affairs.

Find an Al-Anon meeting near you: http://al-anon.org/
Find an Alcoholics Anonymous meeting near you: http://www.aa.org/
Celebrate Recovery a Christ-based recovery program: http://www.celebraterecovery.com/

BIBLIOGRAPHY

Bey, Douglas, M.D. and Deborah Bey, R.N. *Loving an Adult Child of an Alcoholic.* Lanham, Maryland: The Rowman & Littlefield Publishing Group, Inc., 2007.

Cloud, Henry and Townsend, John. *Boundaries: When to Say Yes, How to Say No to Take Control of Your Life.* Grand Rapids, Michigan: Zondervan, 1992.

Cloud, Henry and Townsend, John. *Safe People: How to Find Relationships That Are Good for You and Avoid Those That Aren't.* Grand Rapids, Michigan: Zondervan, 1995.

Drews, Toby Rice. *Getting Them Sober: You Can Help.* Recovery Communications, 1998.

Gass, Justin T., Ph.D. *Understanding Drugs: Alcohol.* Infobase Publishing, 2010.

Grohol, John M., PhD, *Delusion of Grandeur,* PsychCentral, http://psychcentral.com/encyclopedia/delusion-of-grandeur/.

Haroutunian, Harry, M.D. *Being Sober: A Step-by-Step Guide to Getting to, Getting Through, and Living in Recovery.* Rodale Books, 2013.

Hawkins, David R. M.D., Ph.D. *Power Vs. Force: The Hidden Determinants of Human Behavior.* Carlsbad, California: Hay House, Inc., 2002.

"Is There an Alcoholic Personality?" Hazeldon Betty Ford Foundation. http://www.hazeldenbettyford.org/articles/is-there-an-alcoholic-personality.

Jay, Jeff, and Debra Jay, *Love First: A Family's Guide to Intervention.* Center City, MN: Hazeldon, 2008.

Lawford, Christopher Kennedy. *What Addicts Know: 10 Lessons From Recovery to Benefit Everyone.* Dallas, Texas: BenBella Books, Inc., 2014.

Mooney, Al J. M.D. and Catherine Dold. *The Recovery Book: Answers to All Your Questions About Addiction and Alcoholism and Finding Health and Happiness in Sobriety.* New York: Workman Publishing, 2014.

Moyers, William Cope. *Now What: An Insider's Guide to Addiction and Recovery.* Hazeldon, 2012.

Nordqvist, Christian. "What is narcissistic personality disorder?" Medline: Thursday, August 7, 2014. http://www.medicalnewsto-day.com/articles/9741.php

Oscar-Berman, Marlene Ph.D. and Ksenija Marinkovic Ph.D. "Alcoholism and the Brain: An Overview." National Institute on Alcohol Abuse and Alcoholism, July 2004.

Sandor, Richard M.D., *Thinking Simply About Addiction: A Handbook for Recovery.* New York: The Penguin Group, 2009.

West, James W. M.D., F.A.C.S. *The Betty Ford Center Book of Answers: Help for Those Struggling with Substance Abuse and for the People Who Love Them.* New York: Pocket Books, 1997.

Youngerman, Barry, and Heath Dingwell Ph.D., *The Truth About Alcohol.* DWJ Books LLC, 2010.

CONNECT WITH MICHELLE FONDIN

Website: www.michellefondin.com and www.fondinwellness.com

Facebook: https://www.facebook.com/michellesfondin/

Twitter: https://twitter.com/michellesfondin

YouTube: https://www.youtube.com/user/mfondin Join me on YouTube for weekly videos to answer your questions about loving an alcoholic.

Email: michellefondinauthor@gmail.com

The WHEEL of HEALING with AYURVEDA

An Easy Guide to a HEALTHY LIFESTYLE

MICHELLE S. FONDIN

THE WHEEL OF HEALING WITH AYURVEDA: AN EASY GUIDE TO A HEALTHY LIFESTYLE

By Michelle S. Fondin

Ever wondered why you're feeling out of balance, stressed-out, sick, and exhausted, but still can't sleep? Western medicine often ignores the underlying issues that can lead to fatigue, illness, and disease, but there is a way to revitalize your body and mind without drugs or dangerous side effects. Ayurveda, the "science of life," is a complete wellness system that includes all that we associate with medical care — prevention of disease, observation, diagnosis, and treatment — as well as self-care practices that are generally absent from Western medicine. This truly holistic approach considers not just diet, exercise, and genetics but also relationships, life purpose, finances, environment, and past experiences. In this thorough and practical book, Michelle Fondin guides you gently through self-assessment questions designed to zero in on your needs and the best practices for addressing them, such as eating plans, addiction treatment, detoxification, and techniques for improving relationships. She outlines steps you can take, with minimal cost, to heal common ailments such as high blood pressure, heart disease, diabetes, excess weight, anxiety, and depression. These time-tested methods for body, mind, and spirit wellness offer benefits to anyone at any age. ($15.99 New World Library)

THE SECRETS OF THE WHEEL OF HEALING 8-CD AUDIO SET WITH WORKBOOK

By Michelle Fondin

How would you like to wake up every morning feeling phenomenal? Imagine what it would be like to never have to go to the doctor's except for checkups? What would it feel like knowing you could prevent diseases like heart disease, strokes, cancer and diabetes? Heal your life with *The Secrets of The Wheel of Healing Audio Program* that goes in depth with author Michelle Fondin in her interview with radio host, Nick Lawrence. This self-help motivational program is an expansion of *The Wheel of Healing with Ayurveda: An Easy Guide to a Healthy Lifestyle* In This 8-Module Audio Program You Will: 1. Shift your thinking from a victim state of consciousness to an empowered state. 2. Learn about Ayurveda, a 5,000-year old medical system from India. 3. Learn simple ways of eating healthfully without going to extremes. 4. Understand what motivates you in life and start to find your life's purpose. 5. Learn how your mind, body and emotions are interconnected and how your state of mind may be what's making you sick. 6. Feel more connected by nurturing relationships. 7. Learn how a spiritual practice can take you to higher levels of health. 8. Learn why you are feeling overwhelmed and why your mind is chaotic. 9. Learn how to use Ayurveda to stay in balance. This 8-CD set on Ayurvedic Medicine comes with a workbook to help you with your healing, and emphasizes health, fitness and dieting. With over 4.5 hours of listening, you will immerse yourself into Ayurveda. (www. thewheelofhealing.com)